*Christ and
Prometheus?*

Christ and Prometheus?

A Quest for Theological Identity

JAN MILIC LOCHMAN

WCC Publications, Geneva

Cover design: Rob Lucas

ISBN 2-8254-0931-6

© 1988 WCC Publications, World Council of Churches,
150 route de Ferney, 1211 Geneva 20, Switzerland

Printed in Switzerland

Contents

Preface

There is an existential background to this book. If there is anything special about my theological and academic pilgrimage, it is the simple fact that I have taught theology both in Eastern and Western Europe: for eighteen years in the East, at the Comenius Faculty in Prague, Czechoslovakia, and for the same length of time in the West, particularly at the University of Basel, Switzerland. It is tempting to give an account of my "memory and hope" in relation to these different contexts.

Of particular interest is the issue of theological identity within such a pilgrimage. The concept of identity often comes up in contemporary debates. It plays a central role in today's anthropological discussions. It tries to express the deeply human concern for a truly personal humanity liberated as much as possible from external social pressures and patterns of cultural alienation. It focuses on the unmistakable "I" and hopes that human life will become identical with its own authentic vision.

In Christian theology, there is the vital issue of theological identity, the question traditionally raised under the heading of "essence of Christianity" (or *proprium christianum*). Christianity appears in the arena of history as one of many religions and social movements. Theology is one of the many disciplines in the "houses of humanities and sciences" (one faculty among many in classical European universities). Much in Christian life and thought is comparable to other religions and ideologies, · much is historically conditioned. Where is, in the world of many voices and many choices, our *proprium*, the essential unalienable voice of theological authenticity?

There is also the problem of the ecumenical identity of the Christian way. Christians as the pilgrim people of God move through different times and spaces. Necessarily, their faith and their life-styles are coloured and shaped by their different contexts. What has a Christian of the third century in common with us today? What has today's Christian from a Coptic church in Africa to say to a "WASP" sister or brother? It is to be hoped that they *have* something essential in common, they *have* something essential to say to each other. There *is* an ecumenical identity of Christians in time and space. Yet that identity does not lie patently open, it has to be sought for, worked out, discovered and rediscovered. There are distances in time and space, there are frontiers between societies and cultures that have to be crossed and overcome ecumenically. Particularly for a Christian firmly rooted in his or her distinctive traditions and then transplanted into a radically different context, the quest for theological identity becomes a burning issue.

All these three dimensions of the identity issue will be touched upon in this book. However, biographically conditioned, it is the third aspect that will emerge as a "loose thread" holding the chapters together.

In the first three chapters, I try to reflect on some essential experiences from Eastern Europe, particularly from my life in Czechoslovakia. The following chapters will deal with some actual challenges experienced in my present theological and academic work in the West (and in the ecumenical movement). The sections belong together, contributing as they do to my sense of identity in my theological quest. It is a dialectical identity, to be sure, not a rigid, monolithic one; that is, an identity in dialogue with radically diverging situations, responding to different challenges, setting different priorities. You cannot dogmatically repeat in Basel what you learned in Prague. The theological pilgrimage has to pay attention to the new climate and the changed landscape. Ultimately, however, it is the same pilgrimage. You need not forget in Basel what you learned in Prague. On the contrary, the lessons you had to learn there can sharpen your eyes for the dangers and promises of the new situation, e.g., in helping you not to become uncritically captive to the new society and culture. The memory of yesterday can strengthen our hope today.

The title of this book, *Christ and Prometheus?*, highlights one theme in my quest for theological identity. It refers to the issues involved in theological encounters with Marxism. This is, no doubt, a question of ecumenical importance. In the European East, Marxism is an official state ideology attempting to integrate (and dominate) all areas of public life. In the West, I was confronted with a certain revival of interest in Marxism particularly among those segments of community seeking an ideological alternative to the given "establishment". And in some countries of the third world, Marxism became attractive as a particularly sagacious instrument in the struggle for liberation from the structures of social exploitation. Everywhere it is a theological task of ecumenical Christianity to respond to the Marxist challenge.

My attempt at responding to this challenge is primarily rooted in my Eastern European experience. In that particular context there is not much inclination to embrace Marxism as *the* ideology in the churches. Not only because of its declared atheism but also because its official claim to be "the teaching of all teachings and the art of all arts" had been compromised in most directions. Especially in its prevailing rigid and intolerant version it has lost much of its credibility. Yet the same experience showed that it would lead to theological impasse to ignore or to write off the Marxist challenge, and to respond to the intransigent ideology in a spirit of theological intransigence. Christians can learn even from the strange voices, not jeopardizing or giving up their identity by surrendering to their claims. On the contrary, they can strengthen it by witnessing to the sovereignty of the gospel and seeking to encounter their opponents without prejudice. For the gospel of Christ (as my main theological teachers Karl Barth and Josef L. Hromadka kept reminding us) is the gospel *for* the East and the West, the *good news* even for atheists.

The immediate impulse to work on the manuscript of this book was the invitation I had from two distinguished academic institutions. In March 1985 I was invited by the University of Birmingham to deliver the Edward Cadbury Lectures. A few weeks later I gave the Warfield Lectures at the Princeton Theological Seminary.

The lectures given in Birmingham and in Princeton were not identical, yet there was a considerable overlap in what I presented. Both dealt with different aspects of my quest for theological identity. Much of what I said is reproduced in this book.

1.

The Radical Heritage:
Czechoslovak Roots

I begin by identifying that particular confessional tradition which has unmistakably shaped my thought and life: that of the Czech Reformation. I do so not to provide historical information. For me, historical memory has a deeper meaning. It is a part of my actual identity. This is true of every church and theology. They live and move in the "community of pilgrims" — not only in space (in the ecumenical communion with the contemporaries) but also in time (in the communion of faith with the forerunners). A Christian always lives in, and from, the heritage of his or her ancestors.

However, there are times and situations when this acquires a much deeper significance. Tradition is not only a "historical background"; it is formative base, sustaining ground, a source of inspiration and orientation. In Eastern Europe, this is particularly true. The curtains of a relatively "closed society" cannot be completely drawn in its temporal dimension: here, history has a new liberating function. The doors closed in space open in time. Memory feeds hope.

Reformers and martyrs

The Czech Reformation[1] was a multifaceted, dynamic reform movement which, beginning as early as the fourteenth century, reached its flowering in the fifteenth. The term "Hussitism" recalls the key figure of the Czech Reformation, the Prague scholar, preacher and martyr Jan Hus. But the movement was much broader. There was the Unity of the Czech Brethren after Hus, and there was a remarkable reform movement before Hus. One name particularly should be recalled in this connection, that of Jan Milic from Kromeriz (1325-1375). He has been called the "Father of the Czech Reformation"; he had already embodied in his life and work the basic emphases of the movement.

Jan Milic was a church dignitary of high rank and a royal bureaucrat, at a time when the kingdom of Bohemia, with its capital Prague, was unquestionably one of the most important centres of Christian civilization. Prague was the seat of Emperor Charles IV and of the oldest university north of the Alps. Naturally Milic acquired deep insights into the power and glory — and also the manifold corruption — of church and state. He was a biblically committed Christian. The confrontation of the biblical vision with the actual conditions of the church and society led to a personal crisis with far-reaching consequences. Milic gave up his lofty position to become a servant of reform.

Three particular emphases characterized the work of Jan Milic, and they remained the constitutive elements for the whole of the Czech Reformation.

1. There was a strong eschatological motivation and orientation. The vision of the kingdom of God, and still more concretely of the coming city of God, was of paramount importance, not only as a source of private consolation but also as a challenge to the established ecclesiastical and social order. The Book of Revelation received special theological and ethical attention, and its message of apocalyptic judgment, its ultimate promise of "a new heaven and a new earth", the coming "new Jerusalem", became rallying points. The Hussite hope for the renewal of church and society was present already in Milic.

2. The instrument for renewal was the preaching of the word of God. Milic became a passionate preacher. The eschatological vision had to be clearly articulated and guided by the original word of Jesus, and it had to be based on the prophetic and apostolic witness. Milic preached to the educated in Latin, and to the upper classes of Prague society in German. He also addressed the people of Prague in general, using the Czech language. The eschatological hope and task was by no means to be entrusted to the privileged ones, in either the social or spiritual sense. Through the word of Christ, the whole people of God enter into the heritage of the children of God. Milic and his disciples — "the young eagles" as he called them — tried to awaken the consciousness and the conscience of Prague.

3. There was a strong emphasis on the practical ethical consequences of the eschatological witness. The preacher cannot remain in the pulpit. He has to work for practical results. This implies an act of personal conversion. Beyond that Milic raised the prophetic question about new conditions for those converted. It is not enough to proclaim the gospel of the new life, and then to let people go back into the old social conditions.

New structures are needed for the new life. So Milic began a revolutionary experiment. In the centre of Prague he established a foundation for the most despised people in medieval society — the prostitutes — in order to provide an effective new start for them after their conversion. He called that house the "New Jerusalem". An outrageous contrast! Indeed, Milic was promptly accused by the establishment powers and summoned before the pope. He defended his preaching and actions as legitimate and biblical: a clear witness that the "city of God" has something to do with the concrete conditions of our secular cities. The eschatological promise mobilizes Christians to practical response, which has social consequences.

"The father of the Czech Reformation" died while defending his cause in Avignon. He left many "children" in Bohemia. The most important of them was Jan Hus (1372-1415) who reminds one in many respects of Milic. Hus also started out on a most promising career, an academic one. He became one of the best-known professors, and even rectors, of Prague University. But his heart belonged primarily to the truth of Christ. There was no spectacular conversion. Rather there was a long spiritual struggle connected with his theological and philosophical work. Hus participated in passionate disputes at Prague University between the realists and nominalists. Are "universals" (general concepts) names or realities? Hus was a realist — even when, from the point of view of academic debates, this already seemed to be an obsolete position. But he remained a realist less for speculative reasons than ethical ones. For him the question of truth was at stake. What is the truth? This was the key issue for Hus and for the Czech Reformation.

In answering this question, Hus rediscovered the *biblical concept of truth*. To him, truth (*pravda*) was not only intellectual insight into the structure of being (as the Greek *aletheia*), but even more the supporting, challenging, and binding reality of the living God and God's righteousness (*emeth*). To know truth necessarily implies doing it, responding to its vision in obedient action. Ultimately, truth is Jesus Christ. And Jesus Christ is the incarnate word, who calls for the "incarnation" of his words in the life of his church and the world. Theological theory has to relate to reality both in its personal and social aspects. Thus a philosophically realistic view of truth seeks to transform the established order in conformity with the revealed will of Christ.

As a consequence of such teaching, there was an outbreak of reforming zeal, even revolutionary unrest, within the university and the city of Prague. For measured by its apostolic origins, established Christendom appeared in many respects as apostasy; some of its orders flatly contradicted the will of Christ. Hus contrasted particularly the commitment of Jesus, the poor "king of the poor", with the self-centred power and glory of the pope and his church.

As long as the scholar remained within the confines of the university, there were tensions but no open crisis. But Hus could not limit himself to academic teaching. He became a powerful preacher, whose Czech sermons in the Bethlehem Chapel (not far from the place of Milic's New Jerusalem) soon reached the masses of Prague. The authorities, and eventually the pope himself, intervened. A ban was declared against Hus, and an interdict against the city of Prague was enforced.

Hus left the city, but he refused to give up his preaching and teaching. He appealed to Christ; no earthly authority had the right to silence God's truth. So he continued his activities outside Prague, and the masses of Bohemia joined him. This alarmed not only the pope (or the popes, for there was a schism in Christendom) but also the Council which was to meet in Constance. Hus was offered a hearing at the Council, and he accepted.

The Council of Constance was supposed to be an instrument of church reform. But the Czech reformer was too radical for the reformers of Constance, including people like Pierre d'Ailly and John Gerson. They were not willing to listen to his arguments. Against all the assurances of the emperor, Hus was imprisoned and urged to recant. He refused. Hus was not stubborn; he was ready to listen to the arguments of the Council fathers, but only if they corresponded to the truth of Christ. This truth had to be defended even at the cost of one's life. The Council sentenced him as a heretic and he was burned at the stake on 6 July 1415.

But "the blood of the martyrs is the seed of the church". The whole kingdom of Bohemia rose up in his defence. The political representatives protested. The masses of the Hussites defended the Reformation against a whole series of crusades launched against the Bohemians. In 1432 the Hussites came to Basel to defend their case again before the Council, but now as partners, not as the accused. The Council had to acknowledge their Reformation. This was still the Middle Ages, yet in the midst of Western Christendom an alternative church was constituted.

At its beginnings, the Hussite movement was very dynamic both spiritually (the Hussites were well versed in biblical knowledge) and socially. But after years of physical and spiritual wrestling with the powers of the Counter-reformation Hussitism became weakened. The Hussites turned to so-called Utraquism, a reformed church of a strongly conservative character, but still one in which a serious impulse towards biblical Christianity was never abandoned.

The true evangelical inspiration, nevertheless, was represented especially by the *Unitas Fratrum* (the Unity of Brethren) which arose around 1457 out of a handful of determined Christians. They gathered in the small village of Kunvald in East Bohemia in order to build there a real Christian community, one fashioned on the apostolic model. The Unitas Fratrum expanded in Bohemia and Moravia, but they always remained a small minority in the population. Throughout almost all its history it was persecuted. Nevertheless, it presented, in its profound spiritual resources and in its particular cultural achievements, the clearest phenomenon of Czech religious life in the sixteenth and seventeenth centuries. One calls to mind its eminent theologians and thinkers, such as Lukas of Prague, Jan Blahoslav and especially Jan Amos Comenius (1592-1670).

This development of Czech Protestantism applied not only to the Unity of Brethren but also to the Utraquist Church (to which ninety percent of the people belonged). Considerably enriched by its contact with the German and Swiss Reformations, it became even more evangelical. However, the development was tragically destroyed in 1620. The Protestant army and its king, Friedrich von der Pfalz, were defeated in the battle of the White Mountain, near Prague, by the fanatically Catholic Hapsburgs. A ruthless Counter-Reformation, certainly one of the most thorough in all Europe, took its toll in Bohemia and Moravia. The leaders of the evangelical aristocracy were put to death, the evangelical faith was labelled a crime against the state, free citizens were forced to become Catholic or go into exile. Protestant life in Bohemia and Moravia was crippled during the long decades of the Counter-Reformation. For many good reasons, this time was called "the era of darkness".

Finally, after 150 years, (in 1781) the Edict of Toleration was issued by the Austrian Emperor Joseph II, who realized the political and spiritual dangers of oppression and of the open resistance from the underground evangelical groups, especially in Moravia. The edict assured the remainder of the evangelical churches a limited toleration. In spite of the radical operations of the Counter-Reformation, over 70,000 of the "quiet ones in the land" now opted for the evangelical faith. They wanted to hold on to the legacy of the Czech Reformation bequeathed by the Hussites and the Brethren. But that was not permitted, as they could choose only to become Lutheran or Reformed. Thus there grew up in our country a Lutheran and a Reformed church. Both met hard times. During the Catholic rule of the Hapsburgs, both were merely tolerated and for decades not given equal rights. In a real sense, only after the fall of the Hapsburg monarchy in 1918 did they secure equal rights. In 1918 the old wish was finally granted, as both Czech evangelical churches united on the basis of the Czech Reformation. They were now called the "Evangelical Church of the Czech Brethren". A new era of Czech Protestantism had begun.

The Magna Charta of the Czech Reformation

What was the theological shape — the programme — of the Hussite Reformation? It is not easy to give a concise answer to the question. The movement had developed a whole spectrum of different trends and factions, like the radical Taborites, the more cautious Prague party, and later the Czech Brethren. Yet there was a distinct common denominator in the multifaceted movement. All of the main groups among the Hussites subscribed to a common manifesto, the "magna charta" of Hussitism: the *Four Articles of Prague* (1419). They form the basic theological outline of the Czech Reformation.

1. *The word of God is to be preached freely.* First things first. With its first principle, the Czech Reformation pointed to its origins, both historical and spiritual. These origins were identical with the origins of the church itself, in the prophetic and apostolic message of the word of God. In the course of history, the apostolic foundation had become covered by the dust and splendour of ecclesiastical tradition. In many respects, the immediate contact with the biblical message had been interrupted. The free preaching of the word of God was the instrument of its renewal. Both parts of the formulation have to be emphasized. Preaching of the word was to be encouraged, not just interpretation and translation of the biblical texts. To be sure, translation is important, and the Hussites worked on a Czech Bible. Yet the real renewal of faith arises out of a living encounter with the living word, in dialogue between a preacher and a congregation. Both Milic and Hus were masters of such dialogue.

This preaching has to be free. This applies first to the word of Christ; it has to be set free from its traditional confines. It would be wrong to say that the medieval church had forgotten the biblical message. Yet under the authority of its traditional magisterium, this message had been narrowed down. There had been a tendency to monopolize the exposition of the Bible, while the walls of dogmatic tradition were built up around it. The Hussites opposed these developments. The word, Christ himself, will defend its truth. Its spiritual presence in the church cannot be bound to institutionalized conditions. Consequently the freedom of preachers had to be enlarged. There could be, strictly speaking, no monopoly over preaching. It is a universal gift entrusted to the whole people of God. The Taborites went so far as to question the institutionalized office of preachers. Everyone, men and women, may be called to witness. Everyone should have immediate access to the word.

2. *The sacrament of the body and blood of Christ is to be served in the form of both bread and wine (*sub utraque*) to all faithful Christians.* For the Hussites, this second article had been of central importance. In celebrating the Last Supper, they returned the cup into the hands of all communicants. The cup became the symbol of the Czech Reformation. Is this to be understood as a liturgical novelty? Some church historians have tended towards this conclusion: "You do not reform the church and the world by a reform of ceremony" (A. Hauck). Yet this is a deep misunderstanding. For the Hussites (and, I would claim, not only for them!), the Lord's Supper was much more than a mere ceremony. In this sacrament, the main lines of their faith and theology converged. The following three seem to me particularly important.

A. At this very point, the infamy of the established church was blatantly apparent. In withdrawing the cup, church authorities dared to manipulate even the sacramental memory of the death and resurrection of Jesus Christ himself. The realization of the contradiction between the articulated "last will" of Christ and the practice within the church came as a real shock to the Hussites. Their leader after Hus, Jacobellus, said: "All priests are actually the thieves of the blood of Christ." They had reserved that blood for their exclusive use.

B. Here the social implications of the Last Supper became relevant. The blood of Christ is the bond of salvation for all the people of God. It must not be made into a privilege of church officials. In the presence of the Lord, all distinctions dissolve; all the children of God join in their common heritage. All are priests — all are subjects and not just objects of the celebration. The experience of the Christian brotherhood, so strongly felt and grounded in the sacramental community, radiates into all spheres of life. The ecclesiological and social initiatives of the Hussites, particularly the Taborites, are to be understood from this perspective. Therefore the *sub utraque* was more than a ceremonial reform. The cup is in fact the symbol of the eschatological community of women and men.

C. The eschatological aspect of the Lord's Supper was stressed by the Hussites. They celebrated communion as an anticipation and representation of the coming kingdom of God. It is the sacrament of the new age, empowering believers to stand firm and to overcome the temptations and struggles of the old age. Frequently the sacrament was celebrated on mountain tops (the eschatological symbolism is apparent). In this understanding, the Hussites went a different (and possibly more biblical) way than the reformers of the sixteenth century. Much of the spiritual energy of the latter Reformation was devoted to the ontological aspects of Christ's presence in the sacrament; the question of the "elements" and their metaphysical status preoccupied people's minds and debates. The Hussite emphasis on Christ's eschatological presence in the community of believers might actually be closer to the original meaning of the sacrament than the sixteenth-century discussions.

3. *Priests must relinquish earthly positions and possessions, and all should live a life of obedience based on the apostolic model.* This article indicates the ecclesiological consequences of the Hussite programme. What are the *notae verae ecclesiae* (signs of the true church)? "Word and sacrament" is their reply in the first and second articles, as if anticipating the classical position of the Lutheran Reformation. But the Hussites added a very practical concern: an obedient life based on the apostolic model is also a sign of the true church. This was an attack on the life-style and structure of the Constantinian church. It struck at the privileged position of the priests, because in their case the contradiction between apostolic and Constantinian Christianity was especially sharp. Yet more was at stake — all of the church was to be challenged by the apostolic way. The apostles were the disciples of Christ; they followed his way not only in teaching but also in living. The "apostolic model" is the way of service in solidarity, particularly with those who are poor and under-privileged. Likewise a renewal must produce practical and concrete social consequences in church and society. Not only *orthodoxy* (renewal in biblical teaching), but also *orthopraxy* (renewal in personal and social discipleship) was the goal of the Hussite movement.

4. *All public sins are to be punished and public sinners in all positions are to be restrained.* With its last article, the Hussite Reformation demanded moral discipline in all realms of life. This article may sound like legalistic moralism. No doubt there were legalistic tendencies among the Hussites. But at their best, the emphasis on law and discipline went beyond legalism. Like the later Calvinists, the Hussites recognized that real reform of the church and society has structural implications. The moral and legal orders cannot remain indifferent. Among Christians, they should reflect the "law of Christ". This means discipline. Precisely in this article, the Hussite Reformation showed its revolutionary "teeth". It spoke of sinners "in all positions". There is only one order of justice in the

light of the kingdom of God. God's law refers to all classes and all people. There are no positions which can claim special privileges. The Lord is to be obeyed more than the lords, and the lords are to be judged under the supreme authority of the Lord. Not only the church, but also society is to be shaped in conformity with the royal authority of Jesus Christ. *Ecclesia et societas semper reformanda.*

Ecumenical contribution

Our cursory attempt at charting the spiritual and theological territory of the Czech Reformation raises the issue of its theological significance and actual relevance. Did it make a legitimate *ecumenical contribution?* Many theologians and church historians seem to have doubts about this. Traditional textbooks of church history have little to say in this regard. From the perspective of mainstream Roman Catholic historiography, the Hussites — like the Waldensians before them — were typical medieval heretics, although since Vatican II this view has been corrected by some researchers particularly in relation to Jan Hus himself. For most of the Protestant church historians, the Czech reformers are the "little brothers"; they took certain interesting initiatives, but from a truly Reformation stance they are definitely "underdeveloped", mere precursors and heralds of the classical Reformation of the sixteenth century.

I would like to challenge this evaluation. What follows is a plea for more attention to, and appreciation of, the distinctive contribution of the Czech Reformation to Western Christianity. Perhaps I am biased; the Czech Reformation is my spiritual home. But there is more to it than personal bias. There is the strong experience of the theological and ecumenical relevance of this heritage. Let me try to give the rationale for my judgment.

1. The Czech Reformation understood itself as a part of the broader reform movement within ecumenical Christianity. It did not intend to break the unity of the church but rather to renew and strengthen it on its apostolic foundation. When Jan Amos Comenius looked back at its history, he underlined its solidarity with the reform programmes of past reformers, also including among them a few of the popes and councils of the Middle Ages. He highlighted in particular its close affinity with the Reformation of the sixteenth century. In spite of this broad solidarity, however, the Czech reformers have their own distinct theological accents. They were looking for what may be called *radical renewal.*

The word *radical* has two meanings here. It refers to the two aspects which seem to be typical for the Czech Reformation. On the one hand, in their confrontation with the established church, which stood in need of reform, the Czech reformers referred back to the apostolic origins — to the *radix*, the "roots" — of the church. The praxis of the primitive church played a normative role for them; it is held up in their theological declarations, together with references to the sovereign authority of scripture, as an appeal to binding discipleship. In this *memoria apostolorum* they hoped for, and sought to promote, the restructuring and renewal of the contemporary church.

In returning to the church's origins — a step which had parallels in the Reformation of the sixteenth century — the Czech theologians developed the second accent of their radicality. By referring to the apostolic origins, they emphasized the practice of the early church and placed these practical aspects in the foreground. Such an *orthopraxy* is no less important for the reform of the church than an *orthodoxy*; they should not be played off one against the other, nor should they be separated from each other. To know and to teach the truth means to *do* it.

In this connection, the Czech reformers' constant appeal to the example of Jesus, to his law and his actions, played a decisive role. The Czech Reformation turned directly to the Bible, placed it in the hands of believers; and above all, it emphasized the vitally preached word as a challenge to discipleship. In so doing, it gave great importance to the selection of texts. It was the Gospels, primarily the Sermon on the Mount, which received the greatest attention. Without desiring to set up false alternatives, the following distinction could be made: where the later Reformation concentrated its theology on the Pauline message of justification, the Czech focused on the evangelical commandment of Jesus.

This orientation reached its concrete expression with an emphasis which opened the Hussites to the Waldensians: the call to evangelical and apostolic poverty. As is well known, this was the basic motive in the conversion of Valdes; the wealthy merchant embraced voluntary poverty for the sake of discipleship and of credible proclamation. For Jan Milic and Jan Hus too, the reference to Jesus as the "King of the poor" played an important role in the critique of church and society. The true church of Christ is apostolic in the sense that it understands itself as the "church of the poor".

There is a double significance in this: the church first devotes itself to the poor and takes a stand for them. This was practised with revolutionary consequences by the Hussites in particular. And then the church should live in the spirit of poverty: worldly domination jeopardizes and contradicts the inner constitution of the church, destroying the credibility of its word and mission. The Czech reformers challenged the institutionalized life-style of the established church; they showed up the church in its wealth and power interests — e.g. sale of indulgences — as a church in contradiction with itself. In this regard there was a strong polemic accent in the Reformation. But the Hussites and the Czech Brethren did not merely condemn; they put their message into practice, lived out an alternative, taking the person and word of their Lord seriously. The Hussites, particularly the Taborites, attacked the unjust social structures of "Constantinian Christendom" and experimented with "classless models" of a Christian society. The Czech Brethren concentrated on forming the committed fellowship of resolute disciples of Jesus outside the main stream of society at first, radiating the spirit of Christ into the surrounding culture indirectly but effectively. Common to all is the deep conviction that both the personal and social life of Christian people are to be creatively related to the promise and challenge of the coming kingdom of God. As the revolutionary Prague preacher Jan of Zeliv put it: *Status mundi renovabitur* (the state of the world will be renewed).

Some aspects of this type of thinking and acting may seem, from the perspective of several centuries later, to have been too over-enthusiastic, sectarian and unrealistic. There are in them elements of apocalypticism and legalism. Some presuppositions and consequences had to be clarified and examined theologically. This the Reformation of the sixteenth century would do, and its corrections would not go unheard by the churches of the Czech Reformation.

The permanent contribution of this Reformation was thus the emphatic insistence that a true and serious reform of the church must have its social-ethical and social-critical dimensions. Or, to put it another way, the *semper reformanda* must never be applied only to the realm of doctrine and ecclesiastical theory, but also to the life-style and practical engagement of the church, the personal life of the Christian as well as the institutional life of church and society. A biblically radical reform movement has its integral ethical, even political, dimension.

2. In its emphasis on faith's radical relationship to reality, I see the unique feature of the Czech Reformation and its relative "plus" when compared with other reform movements. Was it not a danger of the great reformers of the sixteenth century that their passion for renewal was related too one-sidedly to doctrine and to the inner realm of the church? Of course this is not exclusively so. The Calvinist churches in particular

were not so one-sided. But looking at the Reformation as a whole, the efforts and initiatives tended towards such one-sidedness.

One cannot overlook the ecumenical significance and achievements, for example, of Lutheran theology and church life. However, one should not ignore the gaps and shadows. I am thinking of a certain inadequacy in the area of the practical and social consequences of the Reformation. Luther's one-sided and gruff "no" to the peasants' revolt is symptomatic. I do not wish to under-estimate the complexity of the given historical moment (1525). But how profoundly burdened Protestant church history has been by fear or theological hesitations in regard to the practical and social demands of reformational freedom! The failure of the evangelical churches in the social area is at least in part explained by this.

Within ecumenical Christianity today we are experiencing a veritable explosion of social-ethical engagement, both in Protestant and Roman Catholic churches. Liberation theology is only one example of this. At the same time, in reaction to this engagement, a growing anxiety is being felt in some ecclesiastical and political circles. There is a dangerous process of polarization under way in our churches.

While social involvement by the church is an urgent responsibility in our day, it becomes effective only when it issues from thoughtful and dynamic faith. Here is where theology has an important task. But theology will not be able to fulfill this unless it looks about its own house and searches out sources and models for a new beginning. Some of those traditionally neglected ones might prove particularly helpful. To my thinking, the voice of the Czech Reformation is such a source and model. It belongs to, and it should resound within, the rich polyphony of ecumenical Christianity.

NOTE

[1] For further study of the theological and social profile of the Czech Reformation, the following works can be recommended (in English): Peter Brock, *The Political and Social Doctrines of the Unity of Czech Brethren*, s-Gravenhage, Mouton & Co., 1957; Howard Kaminsky, *A History of the Hussite Revolution*, Berkeley and Los Angeles, University of California Press, 1967; Jan Milic Lochman, *Living Roots of Reformation*, Minneapolis, Augsburg Publishing House, 1979; Matthew Spinka, *John Hus: a Biography*, Princeton, NJ, Princeton University Press, 1968; Jarold K. Zeman, *The Hussite Movement and the Reformation in Bohemia, Moravia and Slovakia (1350-1650): a Bibliographical Study Guide*, Michigan Slavic Publications, University of Michigan, Ann Arbor, MI, 1977; Jarold K. Zeman, *Renewal of Church and Society in the Hussite Reformation*, Moravian Theological Seminary, Bethlehem, PA, 1984.

2.
Churches without Privileges:
Hopes and Frustrations
of Christians in Eastern Europe

My spiritual home is the heritage of the Czech Reformation. My social home (for the major part of my life) was the Czechoslovak society and culture. As a child and teenager, I was still able to enjoy the humane and creative atmosphere of Czechoslovak democracy, founded in 1918 by Thomas G. Masaryk (1850-1937), a great privilege for which I am deeply grateful. However, that social and cultural home was soon demolished. Abandoned by its Western allies, it was destroyed by Nazi Germany in 1938-39.

After the Second World War, we hoped for new life in a renewed state that would be democratically structured and socially reformed. However, by the Yalta Agreement, Czechoslovakia became a part of the Soviet zone of influence. There were hopes that it would be able to serve as a bridge between the East and the West — as a country of Western cultural orientation which at the same time has been traditionally open to the concerns of the European East. These hopes collapsed. In the year 1948, the Communist Party seized power and overthrew the democratic order by establishing a one-party regime.

After my education in Prague, St Andrews (Scotland) and Basel (Switzerland) in 1945-48, I started my theological work in the new society. It was a conscious choice: during the communist coup of 1948, I was still studying in Basel, but I returned and I have never regretted that. Together with my teachers and fellow students I was convinced that a theologian had a clear vocation in the radically changed conditions. There were evident threats and dangers, there were manifold frustrations for Christians in Eastern Europe, but there were also clear opportunities. Theologically this was the time to test and to prove that Christian identity is not to be bound to a particular social and cultural system. What a challenge!

Looking back from the distance of both time and space, how is one to characterize the hopes and frustrations of a Christian theologian in a Marxist society?

Ambiguities of freedom

If one were to construct a world atlas today, in which the extent of external restrictions to religious freedom in various regions of the world were to be cartographically drawn in, then the East European region would no doubt show relatively dark colours. At the same time, it would not turn out to be "totally black" for all East European countries. With regard to religious freedom, there are important differences between one state and another. One can take the two borderline cases, Poland and Albania, as an example. In Poland the (Catholic) church has been able, in spite of ideological pressure, to retain much of its historical privileges, and its present influence could well make some Western church leaders envious. Albania solemnly declared itself as the "first atheistic state in the world" in 1967, and has liquidated all ecclesiastical and religious institutions and destroyed every trace of the public practice of religion.

In spite of these differences, national religious politics has a uniform tendency in all of Eastern Europe. It arises out of a common official commitment to Marxist-Leninism. In its prevailing orthodox setting this governmental ideology includes atheism as an integral component; the attempt is consistently made to bring it to bear on all areas of social life. The constitutions of most of the East European countries contain articles guaranteeing freedom of conscience and religious liberty. Yet the actual situation is different. This is not only because, as in other regions of the world, programme and reality are not in total agreement, but also because the principle of the "proportionality of freedom" is put into practice. Consequently, those who subscribe to the Marxist "scientific philosophy" and those who follow "religious superstition" are not granted the same amount of freedom. The former are to be promoted, the latter to be discouraged.

The Czechoslovak human rights movement "Charter 77" briefly and clearly gives the state of affairs: "Religious freedom... is systematically restricted by dictatorial caprice: through restrictions on the activity of priests over whom the threat of withdrawal or of loss of the state licence constantly hovers; through existential or other retaliations against persons who declare their religious confession by word or deed; through repression of religious instruction, and the like."

Is it then to be concluded that religion and freedom are at the point of death in the eastern part of Europe? Should one consequently consider religious freedom a lost cause? I would not subscribe to such a line of reasoning. At least three considerations speak against it:

a) *Sociological:* However totalitarian a system may be, no one succeeds in totally occupying all the spheres of freedom in a society. Human beings never fit completely into programmed patterns of behaviour. Even under conditions of seemingly fully realized conformity ("normalization") remembrances of freedom (history is a great power in Eastern Europe!) and dreams of freedom keep stirring under the surface.

b) *Anthropological:* Human freedom is misunderstood if one understands it only as a movement "from the outside towards the inside", from external conditions, and not, at the same time, "from the inside towards the outside", as initiatives of freedom by groups and individuals. The citizens are never merely objects; they are also subjects of their individual and political history of freedom.

c) If one thinks about *religious* freedom, then the *theological* motive will come into play: freedom of faith lives *coram Deo*, "with regard to God", and that means from God's grace, not from the grace of a political power. Here is a dimension of freedom which cannot be guaranteed by any political system, but for that very reason cannot be taken away by it either. The name of God as a point of reference, or better, as the clear horizon of our personal and common human destiny shows a *plus ultra* in every situation of our life. It opens up, even in the conditions of bondage, "gaps of freedom" which cannot be closed by any earthly power.

In these theoretical sentences I was trying to reproduce the living experiences of an Eastern European (Czechoslovak) Christian. They indicate that the theme of religious freedom arises not only out of its political-ideological condition, but also out of its deeper human-theological dimension. Today's East European church history is not merely a history of the threats posed to freedom; it is also a history of its preservation and trial.

My theology teacher, J.L. Hromadka from Prague, responding to enquiries by ecumenical guests concerning reduced action possibilities in the churches of Marxist-socialist society, used to say: "We are as free as we dare to make use of our freedom." The statement can be misunderstood; it could be taken to mean that the church's political difficulties in Eastern Europe are minimal. But as a reference to the "other dimension" of religious freedom, it must receive serious attention, especially among us in the West.

Let me refer to my own earlier ecumenical experiences. There were some not-so-pleasant experiences Christians in Eastern Europe had to put up with. Especially in the years of the Cold War, in our limited encounters with Christians in the West we were often regarded as "poor relations". "Poor", not only economically, but also ecclesiastically and theologically. In particular with regard to the "freedom of Christian people". Sometimes it seemed as if (among some Western church people) the interest in losses and restrictions of Christian freedom in the East was greater than in the signs of its preservation. This occasionally awakened doubt among us in the East: which freedom do they actually mean, who speak so much about the "free world", the "free Europe", the "free society" and deplore the lack of freedom in the ecclesiastical situation in the East not always in the spirit of solidarity, but often, on the contrary, in the spirit of their own self-sufficiency?

It is generally understood in the East that Western democratic society and its churches stand for a historically unique and, until today, an unexhausted commission of representing and defending a social order sensitive to the requirements of the citizens' freedom and to human rights. Yet, will this heritage of freedom, above all religious freedom, really be authenticated unless it is grasped not as possession and right, but rather as a commission and duty for the truly free, i.e. through self-critical examination of our concrete use or misuse of freedom? In this perspective, experiences from Eastern Europe would serve not so much as a discouraging example as stimulation for freer and more credible Christian witness in other areas of worldwide Christianity, particularly in the West.

Let me try to sketch the ecumenical meaning of the Eastern European experience.

A narrow way

In the ecumenical context, the churches in Eastern Europe play an outwardly unassuming yet spiritually significant role.

This role is *outwardly unassuming*. Eastern Europe is a region of deeply shattered Christian institutions. The churches have undergone a radical change within the social order. The main emphasis of the change is in the areas of economics and politics, and its overall objective is the reconstruction of the socialist-communist society. It has of course repercussions on other levels, including the ecclesiastical one. The reconstruction is founded on and carried out through rigidly defined presuppositions of an atheistic ideology which perceives itself as the only authoritative ideology for all public domains.

Correspondingly, the social and cultural context of Christians in Eastern Europe has changed. The traditional privileges of the churches — arising out of the preferential position of the churches in culture and society — were taken away. The "end of the Constantinian epoch" is a familiar expression. The alliance between "throne and altar", which had been evident in Eastern Europe, was dissolved. The era of the political, at least the cultural, supremacy of Christendom in Eastern Europe came to an end. The church has become marginal to society. It is more or less tolerated, and wherever possible, only at the periphery, as a remnant from a forgone epoch. And there are situations where it is unmistakably harassed, not only through the state-supported atheistic propaganda, but also through discriminatory administrative measures. Christians no longer determine or project the official image of their countries. They are — in the diaspora of their Marxist-socialist environment — *Christians without privileges.*

What do these changes mean for the life of the church in Eastern Europe? Without doubt, the way has become a *narrow way*. In the first place, the ecclesiastical possibilities are relatively restricted, in comparison to ecumenical areas where the church still enjoys certain privileges. For example, some of the "givens" of ecclesiastical tradition and religious practice — like baptisms, marriages and funerals — which would once bring even non-committed people into the church, are no longer effective in this way. Christians are on the way from a "national church" to a "confessional church". Only those who have made a conscious and personal decision and therefore know what they are doing have remained active in the congregation. This does not mean that the bulk of the population have left the church. Most of them would not prefer to make a pronounced act of officially leaving the church. But they remain on the periphery; they are no longer an active part of the congregation. In this manner, the "confessional Christians" form a minority among the people.

This minority also has no great means of outreach at its disposal. With the exception of the strictly reduced and well-controlled ecclesiastical press, it has no modern mass media of information and propaganda (radio, television) at its disposal. The voice of the church is not made audible at every turn. Their way has really become narrower.

New credibility
The reduced role of Eastern European churches, however, is not without positive spiritual possibilities. Its altered situation does not only mean a loss. In the evangelical image of the "narrow way", there are clear

opportunities and promises. Lost possibilities do not form the total picture of Christian existence in Marxist-socialist countries. There is, for example, the possibility of achieving a *new credibility* for Christian existence.

It cannot be denied that the credibility of the Christian church in the world today — in East and West alike — has largely been undermined. The history of secularization is also a history of the shrinking credibility of Christianity. And Constantinian Christianity is not without blame. The interpenetration of ecclesiastical institutions with the institutions of the society of the day, which was particularly obvious in the various forms of the union of "throne and altar", provided not only an opportunity to exert a dominant influence but also for an unevangelical capitulation. How often did the privileged church stand in its own way and become its own enemy, fettered by false considerations of its own interests as an institution of the given order! And so the gospel was frequently hidden under the bushel — hidden from those very people who, travailing under a heavy social load, had been waiting for the justice of the kingdom of God. In spite of the outstanding achievements of a Christianly inspired philanthropy, the church and its message lost much of their credibility, especially through their failure to meet the social needs of modern industrial society. How many then arrived at the bitter conclusion: The church speaks of God — but God means its privileges and those of its society; it is a community of conscious or unconscious hypocrites.

So it may be that a church which has no longer any privileges, and therefore needs no longer to defend its political interests, can feel freed from its erstwhile captivity. For the post-Constantinian society the Christian need hardly play the role of an opportunist. The only ground for becoming and remaining a Christian in that situation is that of faith. You have nothing to gain by being a Christian. Rather, you lose. And here is the chance of a new credibility. The mere existence of the Christian church can now already be true witness. A community of pilgrims who do not seek to preserve any social privileges or maintain any political clout, who consciously live in the new society and take it seriously — and do so unequivocally as Christians: is not this already — this presence of the Christian community within the Marxist-socialist world — a basic witness to this society?

This possibility is beginning to be realized through some of the most distinctive forms of the churches' activity. It is evident in their *preaching*. For in these congregations, an evidently "poor" and "powerless" word gains a remarkable power. It is certainly not the case everywhere. There are also in Eastern Europe lukewarm congregations and indifferent pastors. And yet, taken as a whole, preaching has become authentic, charged with the power of inner conviction.

This is true also with respect to the missionary witness of Christians in the everyday context of their lives. Such a witness is by no means easy. Very often Christians are surrounded by prejudiced people, even by atheists. They cannot rely on a matter-of-course benevolence. Nevertheless, in one sense this witness is also easier than before. The Christian is "conspicuous", a visible exception. He or she is "questionable" — in a literal sense. The Christian evokes questions. This is not always agreeable. Most people do not like to be asked the most personal, most existential, i.e. the religious, questions. "Religion is a private matter" and too direct questions hurt our "intimacy". Yet for a committed Christian it also involves a genuine missionary chance. If we are asked questions, we have to give answers — and we *may* give answers. This is our chance to speak up and to be heard again. The chance of making a credible witness.

All this particularly involves our lay people. They are the real "apostolic existence today", men and women participating, in solidarity, in the hopes and frustrations of their neighbours and at the same time living without compromise their Christian faith. Yet this new chance to be credible is not the monopoly of lay people. It belongs also to the clergy and theologians. "Clergy" as a sociological group became considerably poorer, both economically and in terms of social prestige. In some countries, the pastor's salary is below subsistence level. A minister or a priest is not a "dignitary" any more. He has to struggle for his existence, especially if he has a family. Yet exactly in this situation he has achieved a new and authentic dignity. There is a visible change. Among the public there was a general distrust of the clergy. In much of the Czech literature of the last century, the clergyman was suspected, and depicted as a hypocrite. The attitude is very different today. The minister or the priest is taken much more seriously, even in the arts and literature. They are, of course, unusual types, conspicuously accountable. But they are now trusted as persons. Their personal honesty and professional integrity are no longer questioned. They have become credible.

What can one learn in the West?

What does the narrow way of Eastern European churches say to the West? What can be learned from the experiences of "Christians without privileges" in the Western — far more privileged — Christendom?

In the West we should first of all simply "learn to learn". That is to say, we must appreciate the fact that we have something important to learn from these "Christians without privileges". This is not easy. For decades, if not for centuries, the trend in ecclesiastical mission and service, especially within the framework of Protestantism, was in one direction: from West to East. There were reasons for such a trend. In Eastern Europe the Protestant churches were poorer and weaker than in the Western countries of the Reformation. They were and are in many respects dependent upon the stronger Western churches. With good reason, the organs of interchurch solidarity like the Swiss HEKS or the Gustav-Adolf-Werk in Germany spent the greater part of their traditional aid in the European East.

This established orientation of relationships, however, gave rise to "Western paternalism", and to the conscious or unconscious presupposition that the Western way was the "normal" way and that the "rich relatives" are qualified to give the "poor" recipes and suggestions. It led not to a common search and dialogue but rather to a "one-way traffic".

We gradually learn in our ecumenical relationships that paternalistic attitudes are, both spiritually and practically, deeply problematic. We must also learn this in our relationships with the Eastern minority churches, and indeed not only in the interest of Eastern churches, but also in the interest of privileged Christendom in the West itself. For, in fact, we in the West have very much to learn from the churches in the Marxist diaspora. No doubt, the changes in the position of the church in society proceed in the two European domains under totally different ideological and cultural presuppositions. The differences are not to be overlooked. And yet the essential questions are not so divergent in the secularized East and West. Is it not true that we too in the West noticeably fall into a diaspora situation? "Diaspora" means "dispersion" and with that a state of affairs is addressed, which is quite typical in many respects for our situation and our life-style. One could almost allude to general sociologically tangible phenomena of modern life, to "dispersion", isolation, indeed dismemberment of neighbourly relationships and associations in our civilization. One quite often lives, and increasingly more, past one another — in the anonymity of residential silos and even in our family homes. This general tendency presents a challenge to Christian congregations.

Have we not also, as Christians in our culture and society, quite progressively become "diaspora Christians"? Indeed, most fellow citizens are still ecclesiastically available on certain occasions; yet, mostly only in a "punctual" way and with long interruptions. Confessing Christians are a minority in the West as well. And if one takes the publicized image of Western society — its mass media and its art — then one often receives the impression that even here the church, in spite of all the possibilities that it has, is to a high degree marginalized. It is not completely different in the West from the situation in the East. Perhaps "over there" are the hard walls of ideological conflict; here rather the elastic rubber barriers of indifference.

In this connection experiences from the East could be of direct importance for us. It could be that the Eastern churches had to vicariously and proleptically go through the experiences which could also be imminent in the West. The chance to ecumenically learn from the already available experiences should for that reason be grasped with openness in our own interest in the West.

What then are the *contents* of the lesson which one could ecclesiastically learn in the West from the East? We can and should learn that the church *can* also live without privileges; that it *must* live without them in certain situations; that it should therefore strive for a *freer attitude* towards the established model of its position in society. I am speaking of a "freer attitude" towards the privileges, not of an arbitrary abandonment of the historically evolved possibilities. Experiences from the East warn us against an enthusiastically radical "flight to the front", or perhaps against a "flight backwards" (to the idealized conditions of pre-Constantinian Christendom). The ideologically forced break of ecclesiastical-political conditions is connected with losses of freedom. The narrow way of the church in the East cannot be considered as a desirable model, not only from the standpoint of the church, but also of society. Threats to religious freedom sooner or later close the space of freedom in other areas of culture and society. This aspect of the lesson from Eastern Europe must not be forgotten in the West.

Yet it would be short-sighted if one were to declare the given ecclesiastical and political conditions in the West as the single acceptable alternative and to absolutize them uncritically, because of the ecclesiastically troubled situation in other parts of Europe. Let us remind ourselves that in all their tribulation the Eastern European Christians go onward with their witness. In the bitter learning process of their narrow way they have not only lost much, but have also gained much, above all the prospect of a new credibility. In this sense their existence poses a permanent question to West European Christians — the question concerning their understanding and practice of freedom. We need not belittle the historically evolved favourable model of the church's position in society, but we should continuously test it as to its load-carrying capacity and be ready to transform it in the interest of a more effective and promising service.

The question to be asked is: *What are we doing with our privileges?* Are we trying desperately, that is, "at any price", to defend them, as if the life of the church were dependent upon the favourable ecclesiastical and political circumstances? Or do we recognize the ambiguity of our political structures and try not to orient ourselves primarily to the "retention of privileges", but rather to measure their significance by their contribution to the effectiveness and credibility of our commission? Are we ready to surrender them if necessary? Above all do we strive not to use the means placed at our disposal through traditional privileges for the expansion of our own position, but rather in the service of Christ and the "least of his brothers" and sisters (Matt. 25:31-46)?

All these questions have very much to do with our personal and common quest for theological identity in the West. We can fulfill our Christian mission only in terms of our concrete here and now — within the given conditions of our specific culture and society. Yet we can do so authentically, in the spirit of freedom and credibility, only if we are self-critically aware that the essential identity of Christian existence requires of us that we do not identify ourselves with the status quo and its pre-established structures. The gospel of Christ transcends all its cultural realizations and captivities. It is the task of theology to remind the church of that fundamental *conditio christiana*. Cautious reflection upon experiences from Eastern Europe could help us not to fail completely in this task. [1]

NOTE

[1] For a more detailed discussion of the situation of Christians within a Communist society see my book *Church in a Marxist Society: a Czechoslovak View*, New York, Evanston and London, Harper & Row, 1970.

3.

Christ and/or Prometheus: Theological Lessons from Christian-Marxist Encounters

How should a Christian church live and react to a situation where the official society considers its very existence as undesirable, and thinks of it as an obsolete remnant from the benighted past and an obstacle to progress? Should the church then cut off its links with the society and ignore its developments, concentrating on its own spiritual life — and hope just to survive? Some churches in Eastern Europe took such an attitude. It would be cheap, and possibly self-righteous, to pass judgment on them. There *are* situations in church history when a ghetto (if not the catacombs) seems to be the only possible mode of Christian existence. There are churches and theologies for which this is a genuine option even in situations where there is no outright oppression: monastic communities, contemplative groups or sects of distinctive life-style in conscious segregation from the broadway of church and society. They emerge as islands (or strongholds) of piety out of the ocean of unbelief; they realize Christian identity in segregation.

However, for the churches of the Reformation, this is an "impossible . possibility". For a church of such radical heritage as that of the Czech Reformation a programme of segregation would mean betraying its own identity. Such a church can be driven into a ghetto from the outside but then it is a state of emergency; it cannot settle down in it, accommodating itself to such a condition. Memory and hope of the kingdom of God push the church towards its society, be it friendly or unfriendly. It makes it a *dialogical* not a monological church, a church of an *open* identity.

But how does it testify to such a vision? How does it practise such a dialogical openness in a Marxist/communist society? That was one of the major concerns of our theological existence in Prague after the communist take-over.

It had taken a long time to prepare for and to open the Christian-Marxist dialogue in Czechoslovakia. Many hesitations and prejudices had to be overcome on both sides. Yet we succeeded step by step. There were small groups of intellectuals gathering unofficially for discussions in private homes. There followed regular seminars at the philosophical faculty of the Charles University under the leadership of Prof. Milan Machovec. There were ecumenical encounters at the Comenius faculty of Protestant theology under the guidance of Prof. J.L. Hromadka. There were international conferences under the auspices of the Academy of Sciences. And there was an explosion of general interest in the later sixties, particularly in the "Prague spring" of 1968, thousands of people eagerly gathering to follow discussions between Christians and Marxists in some of the biggest public halls in the city. Christian-Marxist dialogue became one of the important phenomena in the process for the democratization of Czechoslovak society.

Unfortunately, after the Soviet intervention in August 1968, the organized dialogue was suppressed. The so-called "normalization" process aimed at wiping out every trace of the dialogue. Most of the protagonists (particularly the Marxists) had to leave the country or to resign their teaching positions at the university. Not a single one recanted — an impressive vindication of the spiritual integrity of this experiment.

Is the dialogue dead? Some observers think so. I do not share that view. The Christian-Marxist dialogue did not consist of momentous encounters and happenings only. It was a more sustained movement, surviving the actual events and producing a rich body of philosophical and theological literature. A "mutual interpellation" among Marxists and Christians had been realized. Processes of reorientation had been launched. These can be slowed down but not completely undone and forgotten.

What are the *theological lessons* from the dialogue? Let me try to give a personal account of my experiences. I shall do so under the heading "Christ and/or Prometheus?". This catch-phrase symbolizes and summarizes my understanding of both convergences and divergences in the dialogue that has gone on.

The Marxist saint

Prometheus is the great saint of the Marxist tradition. In response to a question put to him by his daughter, Karl Marx had to name his favourite hero. He said without hestitation: Prometheus. This was by no means a capricious answer. Prometheus had always played an important symbolic role in his thought. He was attracted by different aspects of this titanic figure of Greek mythology and tragedy.

First, Marx appreciates the *rebellious achievement* of Prometheus. This Titan breaks through the realm of the gods. He does so not from personal motives but in the interests of humankind. He brings the fire back to the earth and teaches people to build houses and to establish human settlements.

Secondly, Marx sympathizes with the *martyrdom* of Prometheus. Punished by the jealous gods, the hero is condemned to suffer in chains. His lot symbolizes for Marx the situation of the proletariat. This enslaved class, for him, is a modern Prometheus.

Thirdly, Marx admires the *unbroken spirit* of this martyr for the human cause, particularly his consistent refusal to submit to the pressures of the oppressing gods. Aeschylus's tragic version of the Promethean myth is often quoted: "I hate each and every one of the gods."

It is this rebellious but self-sacrificing and suffering hero who is for Marx from the very beginning of his philosophical work "the most outstanding saint and martyr in the philosophical calendar", as he states in the preface to his philosophical dissertation.[1]

Prometheus became a characteristic symbol not only of the thought of Karl Marx but of Marxian humanism in general. Several years ago, in the German Democratic Republic, a widespread public discussion on the difference between the socialist and capitalist images of the human person was conducted under the alternative symbols of Prometheus and Cain. The same thought was also strong in the new types of "Marxist Christology", in the writings of Vítezslav Gardavsky and Ernst Bloch.[2] For Bloch (as for Bacon), Nietzsche, and Marx, Prometheus represents the "glory of activity" (Nietzsche) and the titanic thrust of the "exploring human spirit" (Bacon). He is a human genius moving beyond all the set boundaries, questioning all the traditional prerogatives of the gods, and installing the human being as the responsible agent and final hope of the universe.

The fundamental issue between Marxists and Christians concerns the question: *Is there a place for Prometheus in the Christian calendar?* Are the biblical-Christian and the Promethean-Marxist perspectives of human nature and destiny mutually exclusive? Is Christ the antipode of Prometheus? If Christ and Prometheus were two exclusive alternatives, then the only responsible encounter between Christians and Marxists would be in terms of confrontation and not dialogue.

For generations, Marxists and Christians have assumed that there is indeed such an "either-or" between Jesus and Prometheus. For Marxists, the Christian concept of salvation as founded in the coming of the Son of God was a myth. Christ as the Lamb was an anti-revolutionary symbol of submissive acquiescence and the word of the cross, with its emphasis on suffering and patience, was the "opium of the people". Christians, on their part, considered the Promethean way as anti-Christian; in it commitment to God has been replaced by commitment to the human. The grace of God's condescension had given way to the assertion of human hubris; the prerequisite of repentance to enter the kingdom of God had given place to the revolutionary transformation of human kingdoms. These options opposed each other, and there could be no compromise between them. "Anathema" rather than "dialogue": that was the prospect.

The developments in Christian-Marxist encounters, and in particular the discoveries of the relevance of the biblical heritage, reopened the debate about the place of Prometheus. They took us out of anathema to dialogue. And in the course of the dialogue, both the converging and diverging elements of Christian and Marxist thought emerged with new clarity.

The Promethean challenge to theology

There *is* a place for Prometheus in the Christian calendar. Both biblically oriented Christians and Marxists seem to arrive at this conclusion. They go even further: there is a better place for him there than in any other calendar, including his own — that is, the Greek tradition. This applies to Prometheus even as a mythological figure. It is significant to notice that in the mainstream of classical antiquity, Prometheus got a rather "bad press". He was a tragic figure, a great pioneer and benefactor of humankind. It was possible to sympathize with him. But ultimately he was a trespasser. He dared to challenge the eternal laws and the ontocratic, that is cosmically pre-established, hierarchical order. Consequently, he was sentenced and punished. The cruel sentence was hardly questioned by the Greeks. Zeus was ultimately right. It is not proper for mortals to transcend their allotted place and endanger the ontocratic harmony.

The Marxian attitude to Prometheus was unthinkable in classical antiquity. It shows a radical change in world-view, the emergence of a new conception of the role of human creativity within the order of creation. This owes much to biblical thought where Prometheus could find a new context. Paul Ricoeur writes: "Unlike Greek wisdom, Christianity does not condemn Prometheus. For the Greeks the fault of Prometheus was that of having stolen the fire of technology and of the arts, the fire of knowledge and of consciousness. Adam's fault is not the fault of Prometheus, his disobedience does not consist in being technical and scientific man; rather, it is to have broken in his human adventure the vital link with the divine."[3]

Ricoeur is right. The biblical God is not a Zeus, and does not impose eternal limits on human beings as on potential competitors. God does not use mythological or ontological chains to keep them bound to an unchangeable spot in the universe. God is not a cosmological policeman jealously watching the frontiers of the unapproachable divine realm. On the contrary, the biblical God creates human beings "in his own image". God considers them not as potential rivals but genuine partners in a covenant. Thus God does not keep the "fire" of creation for divine use, but shares it with human beings. In fact God shares God's very self. In Jesus Christ God goes the way of human beings so that human beings might go God's way, to have life and to have it in abundance, to participate in the life everlasting, the "world without end".

If the biblical God is no Zeus, the biblical concept of humanity is not like the Greek one either. Human beings are not bound to occupy without reservation a place within the preordained structures. They are the children of and heirs to their Father (Gal. 4:7). Their final point of reference is not the once-given order of the cosmos or of society, but the Creator and Redeemer of those structures. Human beings are not only a part but also a counterpart of the creation. They exercise the right of the *dominium terrae*, dominion over the earth. They are called to use and to foster the "fire" of creation in nature and history. They are free, creative, transcending beings. Theirs is an "eschatological existence", challenging the "status quo", changing the world, seeking the "greater justice" of the coming kingdom.

In all this, human beings run the risk, and create the risk, of misunderstanding and misusing their freedom. They are a continuous threat to nature and to humanity. Human beings are sinful creatures. The Bible has no illusions about the real "human condition". And yet, it has no delusions either. In the biblical perspective, the Promethean character of humankind is not tragic and sinful in itself. It is, in spite of all the dangers and temptations, a genuine, unique gift and possibility. If for the Marxists Prometheus stands for humankind as the creative subject of history, for revolutionary humanity, then there is no doubt that there is a place for him in the Christian calendar as well.

For Christian theology this thesis cannot remain a simple affirmation. It is indeed a challenge to give that place to Prometheus in our thinking. This does not happen as a matter of course. Looking into the mirror presented to us by the Marxists, we have again and again to concede that the Promethean element, the dynamic aspect of our own radical heritage, had been notoriously neglected and largely eclipsed. The severe Marxist criticism of religion as the "opium of the people", as "false consciousness" and manipulated consolation, has much to do with the Christian church losing the prophetic and apostolic vision with its concern for total salvation, peace, and justice in history. In both its versions, orthodox and liberal, the church tended to replace that vision by a religion of otherworldliness and inwardness. The Marxist criticism of such a church poses a legitimate challenge. The voice of Promethean atheists was often rude and one-sided. But it brought back to our attention some important aspects which should have received a better hearing in the church if the church is to be faithful to its authentic being.

It seems that these aspects do get a better hearing in today's theology and ecumenical practice. We have no illusions about the state of the church and theology today. They are in many respects in a critical state. Yet one of the hopeful signs is a process of reorientation in academic theology and within the ecumenical movement. The work of great theological pioneers such as Barth, Bonhoeffer, Niebuhr, and Hromadka brought to the fore exactly many of those neglected elements of the radical biblical heritage. Ecumenical thought and action have moved with growing intensity in a similar direction. The "Promethean elements" are taken more seriously. Sometimes it seems that they have even become a new fashion. "Theology of hope", "theology of liberation", "theology of revolution", "political theology" — all these indicate a trend in this direction.

And yet, the Promethean challenge remains and the process of reorientation should go on and result in ecumenical action if it should become more than a "fashion" in theological reflection. Let me give three instances where the Promethean challenge seems to be valid and urgent for our theological orientation.

1. There is a place for Prometheus in our *teaching about God*. We have already said that there is a fundamental difference between Zeus and the God of Abraham, Isaac and Jacob, the Father of Jesus Christ. In Greek thought, gods and human beings are distinguished by their metaphysical status: they occupy different levels of the ontocratic order. There is an "upper realm" of the immortals, and a "lower realm" of mortal human beings. Thus an unchangeable "class structure" separates gods from human beings. A revolt against this structure is self-defeating and

improper. The "upper class" may be resented, the insurgence of the "lower class" may be sympathized with, but the order itself is unchangeable. This is the tragedy of Prometheus.

There is a basic difference in God's relation to humanity according to the Bible. The very element of the encounter is different. It does not occur in a "space relation" of a "double realm" parallelism, but it occurs in an eschatological "time relation" in history. The form of the relation is different. It is characterized by soteriological participation and not by ontological separation. The concern of the biblical God is not with the preservation of a metaphysical wall of partition between immortal and mortal but the integrity of mutual sharing in the relationship of covenant and love. Also, the content of this relation is different. The God of biblical faith does not intend to keep human beings in their place in ontocratic chains; the God of the exodus and the resurrection opens up the way out of all human captivity, even the captivity of death. God is the God of freedom, the liberating God.

Thus the "Zeus-Prometheus" model of the divine-human relationship is radically overcome in the biblical perspective. Oppressive, authoritarian "class" structures determining the relationship between God and human beings are overthrown. The emancipation of humankind is not an affront to this God, but a basic concern. There *is* a place and a role for Prometheus in the scheme of this God.

The lessons from the Christian-Marxist dialogue indicate that the question of God remains one of the most serious stumbling blocks in the way of mutual understanding. There is indeed a genuine divergence between Christians and Marxists at this point, as we shall see later. But there is also much unnecessary confusion. Marxists generally think of God in terms of the Zeus image, a heavenly model of the oppressive class structure. Consequently, atheism opens the way to human emancipation. For the older Marxists, this was a dogmatic tenet; much of their atheistic propaganda was founded on it. The modern Marxists, such as Bloch and Gardavsky, know better; they have reopened the issue of transcendence. Ultimately, however, even for them the idea of God remains an alienating concept.

How then do we proceed? How do we explain this "blind spot" to these otherwise clear-sighted interpreters of the Bible? The theologians should themselves take part of the blame. *They* should have known better. How often in traditional theology has the doctrine of God been shaped more according to Greek and oriental ontocratic models than on biblical Christology. The Holy Trinity, the God of communion and sharing, was confused with an authoritarian God-concept. Traditional theism is not without guilt in this development. It tried to integrate the biblical God into the context of Greek philosophical tradition. It reserved for God the highest level in its ontology. It did so with the best of intentions, but it made God captive to a historically conditioned hierarchical world-view. This fostered the impression that the God of the church is also an a-human superstructure imposed on humanity from above. Many of the "Promethean people" were consequently alienated from such a God and such a religion. It is an urgent task for theology today to clarify the issue, to part ways with the authoritarian concept of God and to rediscover the authentic, liberating, biblical vision of God in Christ.

2. There is a place for Prometheus in our *doctrine of evil*. I do not mean that Prometheus should get more attention as an example of the Fall and the mystery of evil. He has already got too much attention in this respect. Very often in traditional dogmatics the doctrine of sin was based on a "Promethean model". The Fall was interpreted as an act of *hubris*. The content of the hubris was certainly not simply taken over from the Promethean mythology: hubris was not conceived as consisting in the insolence of bringing down the fire of technology. However, the act of transcending the limits and of intrusion into the divine realm was defined as *the* form of sin.

There is some justification for such a definition. It is a normal temptation of human beings to consider themselves as the supreme authority over good and evil. Such a temptation is sinful not only in Greek thought but also in biblical perspective. The tower of Babel represents a perverted movement, not as an act of constructing a secular city but as an act of pretension to construct a tower "reaching into the heavens". Traditional dogmatics is right; there is a revolt which is sinful before God.

The temptation of traditional dogmatics and of traditional piety consisted in generalizing hubris as *the* evil. Such a generalization corresponded much more with the Greek world-view than with the biblical message. It is based on an ontocratic concept of God. In biblical theology this presupposition is eliminated. If God is revealed as the God of the exodus and the resurrection, then sin cannot be understood only as hubris. In the light of Christ, sin is not only the claim *eritis sicut dii* (you will be as gods) which is judged and revealed in its futility; sin is also the opposite temptation: to ignore the liberating engagement of God in the history of human beings and to refuse to participate in God's acts of liberation.

Not only *hubris* but *inertia* also is a basic form of sin. There is a sinful captivity, individual and institutional, persisting within the given structures of thought, morals, politics and economics. There is a sinful "laissez-faire" attitude, a sinful neutrality and non-involvement. In the eschatological perspective, the sin of human beings may primarily lie in an attitude of non-involvement. It is not by chance that the New Testament passes severe judgment on the lukewarm, the non-committed. Theirs is not a less dangerous form of atheism than that of the Promethean atheists. Not only a titanic revolutionary but also a complacent liberal may be in a "state of sin".

The sin of inertia has received much less attention in the churches' theory and practice than the sin of hubris. This has led to serious consequences. The concentration on hubris created an atmosphere in many of our churches, especially in Europe, in which the Promethean move towards emancipation was suspected as a basically sinful move. On the contrary, obedience to given authorities was identified as virtue. "To be calm is the first duty of a citizen." From an eschatological point of view, such an attitude appears as highly one-sided and questionable. The bias against Prometheus cannot be justified. Theological reorientation is needed also in the doctrine of evil. Marxian Promethean Christology is a genuine interpellation in this respect.

3. There is a place for Prometheus in the Christian message of *grace and justification*. The theme of grace is a controversial issue between Christians and Marxists. For Christians, this is the central insight of biblical faith. It is the affirmation of a radical hope which transcends all our achievements and failures because it is grounded in God. For Marxists, this is a dangerous doctrine which easily degenerates into a reactionary ideology of quietism: it suggests that it is not so important to act in history because there is the ultimate heavenly solution to all our problems. The crucial question indeed is: Is grace an alternative to human endeavour? Is theology of justification opposed to the philosophy of work? Does the perspective of grace undermine the human quest for creative self-realization in history? In that case there is no place for Prometheus in a spirituality of grace.

In the biblical understanding grace in no way excludes or depreciates human activity. On the contrary, grace opens up new and unexpected possibilities for action in history. It mobilizes human creativity. It is indeed a hopeful thrust towards a "plus ultra" and, in this sense, a driving force for a "Promethean existence". Father Gonzales Ruiz, a Spanish

Catholic theologian, was right in responding to the Marxist criticism of grace: "Grace is not an intrusion which is to eclipse the epic grandeur of Prometheus."[4]

However, the Marxist distrust of the doctrine of grace is not just misunderstanding. It points to a certain kind of Christian preaching which indeed is "anti-Promethean" and does scant justice to the biblical unity of grace and action, of prayer and work. There is a practice of "cheap grace" in our churches and popular piety. "Cheap" indeed is grace without consequences, faith without works. Dietrich Bonhoeffer was right in recognizing in such an attitude a specific Protestant temptation. This temptation is connected with the classical Reformation teaching about "justification by faith alone". The teaching is sound. There is no other foundation for our hope in life and after than the grace of God. *Sola fide — sola gratia* is indeed an *articulus stantis et cadentis ecclesiae*, the article on which the church stands or falls.

However, in that properly emphasized little word *sola* lies also a danger. It can be misunderstood as suggesting an abstract, "solitary" conception of grace, grace and faith as lofty spiritual entities separated from the other realms of life, particularly from ethical and political responsibility. And so an ominous "hierarchy of truths" emerged. The truth of faith was elevated beyond the truth of works, the truth of justification beyond that of sanctification, the truth of Paul beyond the truth of James. Protestant piety tended to become a "one-dimensional" religion of a spiritualistic and individualistic orientation. Thus the eschatological dynamics of the life of faith was eclipsed and with it the emancipatory implications of grace for the broader strata of human life. It is typical that in the ethical field, the *sola gratia* accent has been applied generally as a critical principle "watching the works" (Fr Gogarten), that is, unmasking human pretensions and utopias, and not so often as positive encouragement to venture a *novum* in the promise of grace.

The encounter with the Marxist critique of biblical thought may help reorient our theology in just this respect. The scepticism of Marxists concerning the doctrine of grace is a warning not to take the emphasis on grace as an excuse for quietism. Their high evaluation of human work and revolutionary activity reminds us of important elements in our biblical heritage. Their critique is certainly one-sided and cannot be accepted without reservations. Their bias against Paul and the doctrine of justification distorts the biblical perspective; yet, they articulate an important stream of biblical tradition. They remind us with challenging emphasis of a genuine biblical truth: "Faith without works is dead" (James 2:26). In this sense, there is a place for Prometheus in the very heart of Christian faith.

Demythologizing Prometheus

The dialogue about the place for Prometheus has brought about a significant convergence between some Christians and Marxists. There has also crystallized a clearer realization of a genuine divergence between the two. This divergence appears as soon as the question is asked: How do we define *the place of Prometheus*? How do we understand his role? Is the Promethean way to be interpreted as the ultimate hope and the salvation of humankind, or is Prometheus the symbol of a meaningful yet strictly secular human engagement? Is he to be understood as saviour or as pioneer?

The classical Marxist answer is inclined to emphasize the ultimate *saving* quality of the Promethean way. The Christologies of Gardavsky and especially of Bloch are typical of such an interpretation. For them, Prometheus is the "saint of rebellious human salvation".[5] The Promethean Christology reveals the ultimate mystery and hope of history: Promethean humankind, progressing towards ultimate self-realization, established itself as the proper heir to the biblical promises of salvation. The kingdom of Promethean humanity fulfills and replaces the expectations of the kingdom of God. *Eritis sicut deus* (you will be as God) — this Promethean dream is more than a dream: it is the real future of liberated humankind. The salvation is at hand: in *our* hands.

Not all Marxists express their Promethean vision in such inspired language as Bloch. However, their response to the question about the place of Prometheus is basically the same. This applies to Karl Marx himself. Prometheus symbolizes for him the essential accents of his historical materialism. This theory is basically philosophy of work, ideology of revolution, with a specific concept of atheism implied therein. Thus the content of his Promethean humanism is best illustrated by these aspects of the Marxian theory.

1. Marx's philosophy is fundamentally *philosophy of human work*. The emphasis on work characterizes his economic system. The work of humankind for him is the only real source of economic values. This is also the main thesis of his anthropology. Work is the authentic expression of humanity. The human being is essentially a "working creature". In his or her capacity to work lies the *proprium humanum*, the specific difference from other creatures. Above all, work is the ultimate basis and hope of universal history. The community of the working class is the real

subject and agent of history. Its creative activity is the driving force of all progress. To be sure, work is also the ground of the human predicament; if the structures in which it is expressed are perverted, as is the case in a class society, human beings suffer. Under the domination of private property work is alienated and this is the cause of all human misery. When the oppressive structures have been broken, the creative activity of people will eventually emerge in triumph and emancipation. And this will be not only human triumph and liberation; for Marx, it has implications also for the universe. The ontological cleavage between nature and history, between matter and spirit, between object and subject will be bridged through the creative work of the human community. Thus the ultimate "metaphysical" issue will be resolved. The hope of eschatological reconciliation, the prerogative of God in traditional theology and philosophy, will be realized by the healing and saving activity of Promethean humanity.

2. The Marxian *concept of revolution* points in a similar direction. As work, revolution is a concrete event in history. Marx analyzes the historical and social conditions of revolution. Later he develops a precise and effective methodology of revolution. But his political philosophy becomes influential not only as a methodology but also as a "gospel of revolution". Socialist revolution is for Marx not only a political act; it is also the opening of ultimate human possibilities. The overthrow of unjust economic structures inaugurates a process of universal healing. The elimination of private property and its domination over the working class sets the end to all types of human bondage. Through the self-realization of working people the fulfilment of nature and history will be achieved. As work, revolution too has a "soteriological" dimension. The Promethean way is the way of secular salvation.

3. In this light, the problem of *Marxist atheism* appears in new perspective. In our preparations for dialogue with Marxists, we often discussed the question: Is atheism a substantial and integral part of Marxism or is it rather accidental and historically conditioned? We generally tended to say it is "accidental". In a sense we were right. We were right in pointing out that the atheism of Karl Marx was clearly a reaction to the prevailing attitude of the Christian churches of his time. Their individualistic piety and their support of the given class-structure justified the denunciation of religion as the "opium of the people". We were also right in reminding our churches that atheism is not the whole of Marxism and that, therefore, as Christians, we must not use the argument of atheism as a pretext to dismiss the challenge of that radical philosophy.

There is indeed a sense in which atheism is accidental and not the "substance" of Marxist thought.

However, we should not overlook that, in a deep sense, this philosophy is consciously and organically an atheistic creed. It is not just inconsistent if even the modern and biblically interested Marxists like Gardavsky and Bloch emphasize their atheism. Gardavsky is very outspoken in this respect: "I do not believe in God even if this is absurd"[6] — the first and the last sentence of his book. Bloch develops his most elaborate biblical interpretation around a dialectical thesis: "Only an atheist is a good Christian; only a Christian is a good atheist."[7] Some of their theological partners reproach them for a certain inconsistency in this respect. Yet they are basically right. If the final hope of humanity is in a kind of Promethean salvation, then there is no real place for the biblical God. Perhaps this God is not quite dead — that is, the question about God is by no means a nonsensical one. Biblical theology makes sense for these Marxists. However, it makes sense as a symbolic expression of Promethean potentialities, of the ultimate promise and hope of human work and human revolution. The keys of salvation are firmly in our hands. The Marxist Prometheus enters into the inheritance of the God of Jesus Christ.

This conception of the place of Prometheus is incompatible with the Christian understanding. In Christian perspective, the hope of salvation is inseparably connected with the one name of Jesus Christ and with what this name stands for, that is, with the liberating involvement of the God of Abraham, Isaac, and Jacob. He is the God of the exodus and the Father of Jesus Christ. His hope of salvation means history; it is, however, not the outcome of history. It mobilizes human energy and work; it is, however, not the sum total of that energy and work. It inaugurates an eschatological *revolution*; it is an *eschatological* revolution: the possibilities of the Ultimate are not our ultimate possibilities. In one sentence: The hope of our salvation is in the liberating *transcendence of God's grace.*

The emphasis on the transcendence of grace as the final dimension of human life is the essential point in which Christianity and Marxism part ways in the interpretation of the biblical heritage. It would certainly be a simplification to fix the border line between Christians and Marxists as the line between atheists and theists. Important attempts at the reinterpretation of these concepts were undertaken in both camps. We pointed to the shifts in emphases among both parties. Many Christians refuse to be identified with the theistic-ontological structures of traditional expressions of their faith in God. Some Marxists elaborate a new concept of dynamic atheism which is not a closed metaphysical attitude any more. These changes are significant because they open new possibilities of mutual understanding. Yet exactly in the course of dialogue, the question about the transcendence of God's grace acquired a new actuality. Marxism disavows this question. It sees in it an improper turning away from concrete human obligations. In view of the misuse of religion in the course of history, Marxism has solid grounds for its atheism. Dedication to Promethean refashioning of this world must not be watered down with "pious reasons". Christians should fully understand that too. We are called to a self-critical *metanoia* (rethinking) in this connection. How often our emphasis on transcendence meant alienation from our historical and social responsibility! Yet in readiness for such a theological *metanoia*, the obligation of Christians to bear witness to the transcendence of God's grace must still continue.

This transcendence does not alienate human beings in their historical and social existence. It reflects the work of God in the life of Jesus of Nazareth. Thus it does not ignore, but radically confirms the importance of the historical and social dimension of human existence. At the same time, however, it asserts that the secular dimension is not the only and ultimate dimension. We are not "one-dimensional" persons. Here lies the danger of ideological atheism. If God is ideologically denied, then human beings tend to be dissolved in the processes of nature and history. They become imprisoned in their immanence and in their secular projects. The penultimate becomes ultimate for them. Their total destiny then depends on their accomplishments. They live with the possibilities of happiness and euphoria in the moments of their success. But they also live under the law of frustration and despair in the face of defeat and guilt.

The Christological message of the transcendence of grace liberates us from this tension. It witnesses to the *transcendence*: human beings are never used up completely in their social and historical conditions. There is a radical "plus ultra" in all our situations. And the Christian message speaks of *grace*: our salvation does not depend on the success or the failures of our efforts. What is ultimate is not our accomplishment. The ultimate is not our failure and not even our death. The only ultimate, our eschatological future, is grace.

We have already emphasized that this perspective of the transcendence of God's grace does not eclipse the "epic grandeur of Prometheus". It demythologizes that grandeur but in such a way that it installs Promethean humanity in its own right. It is not burdened with a soteriological mission. It does not have to perform this "mission impossible". Our work is a secular activity and not an act of self-redemption. Our social involvement is participation in historical liberation and not the work of messianic salvation. We need not construct the new Jerusalem. We should build up, in the light of the new Jerusalem, our secular cities.

Thus the transcendence of God's grace does not confound but rather clarifies the Promethean concern. Very often human life is endangered by a *false absolutization* of human activities and by tragic messianic claims. Marxism has been notoriously tempted to do this. Often it has presented itself as doctrine of secular salvation. In some situations this pathos was its strength. It was also its danger. In such an approach, the secular reality of human world, particularly the political reality, becomes mythologized. Political issues appear as matters of ultimate concern. Political history becomes "religious" history. Political organization presents itself as an avant-garde of the absolute future. Political ideology takes on the traits of an untouchable dogma. Political action turns into an eschatological struggle. Consequently, the political opponent is understood and treated as an apocalyptic enemy. Through these forms of "mythologization" the human dimension of political life is eclipsed. Politics, this genuine human concern, loses its proper secular character. It tends to become de-humanized.

Facing this danger, Christian demythologization of Prometheus may serve a legitimate political concern. Refusing to take Prometheus as saviour, the Christian can still support him as a pioneer of secular emancipation. Promethean salvation is a myth; Promethean involvement is possible. In other words, politics under the aspiration *eritis sicut deus* is a tragic misunderstanding of human condition and a hopeless hubris. Politics under the promise *eritis sicut homines* (you will be as human beings) is a meaningful and urgent task for all of us. That humanizing task, says the young Karl Marx, is "to change all the conditions under which man is an oppressed, enslaved, destitute, and despised being".[8] This is a genuine Promethean mission. Christians and Marxists, together with all people of good will, should share in it.

What is man?

Let me conclude this chapter about the place of Prometheus by recalling a personal episode. While walking about the campus of Harvard University, I noticed the inscription on the library building: What is man that thou art mindful of him? I enquired about the decision to inscribe these well-known words of the psalmist on the wall of a university building. I was told that originally there was a different suggestion for the epigraph. It was the famous saying of Protagoras: *Panton metron anthropos* — man is the measure of all things. However, the university representatives preferred the psalmist to the philosopher.

This is a good illustration and summary of our discussion of the theological lessons to be learned from the Christian-Marxist encounters. What is the ultimate meaning of human life? Where is the true dignity of the human being ultimately to be found? The sentence from Protagoras gives an answer: Man is the measure of all things. These words may be interpreted in different ways. In modern times, one tendency of interpretation has become particularly strong: that is, as a programme of human emancipation from a given social and metaphysical order. This is an emphasis of the renaissance and post-renaissance humanism with its pathetic admiration of the human dignity: "Glory be to Man in the highest! for man is the master of things" (A.C. Swinburne).

Karl Marx also is to be seen in this tradition. He is certainly free from the enthusiastic optimism of many of his humanistic predecessors. He is more conscious of the ambiguous character of the human world. He knows of the presence of the antithesis in the dialectical process. He realizes and analyzes the depth of human alienation. Yet he has no doubts about the final perspective. Ultimately history moves towards the resolution of its contradictions. It moves towards fulfilment in a post-revolutionary society of free men and women. In this sense "man is the measure of all things" is also a Marxian expression of both the dignity of humanity and of the humanity-guided hope for nature and history.

Let me confront this vision of the nature and destiny of human beings with that other option: "What is man that thou art mindful of him?" In these words, the ultimate hope of humanity is not founded in the habitus or achievement of human individuals or collectives; human hope is grounded in the "mind of God", or in the "transcendence of grace". Words like "mind of God" sound idealistic. They were often interpreted in this sense. But that is to misunderstand the psalmist. Biblically the "mind of God" was revealed in the covenant of God, particularly in the two central events of the Old and New Testaments, the exodus from Egypt and the resurrection of Christ. Both these events are acts of liberation and revolutionary openings in history. Thus the psalmist's word is by no means a "magna charta of quietism". These events are acts of *God's* liberation. In God is the ground for our dignity and hope.

How does this conception relate to the *panton metron anthropos* thesis? At first glance there seems to be an outspoken contradiction. However, if we put the biblical word into its proper context, the situation changes. It is taken from Psalm 8. The psalm continues: "Yet thou hast made him little less than God, and dost crown him with glory and honour. Thou hast given him dominion over the works of thy hands; thou hast put all things under his feet..."

This is a dynamic text and no simple denial of the thesis that "man is the measure of all things". On the contrary, for the psalmist also human beings are a measure of all things. They are this measure in a very dynamic sense. They are the stewards of creation, God's plenipotentiaries, the shepherds of the universe. There is no tendency here to contain, restrain, or temper down human creative responsibility. Hence there is a place for, and there is a praise of, human work and creativity. And yet, clearly, a different answer is given by the psalmist to the ultimate question. The final dignity and hope of humankind do not rest on our unique role and achievement in the universe. They are in our place within the mind, the covenant, of God.

How are we to understand this assertion? I understand it as the fundamental assurance of the biblical faith that human beings are not left alone with their tremendous task in this universe, that they live, create, fail and die within the context of that strange love by which they were created and on which they may rely. Here is their *centrum securitatis*, their final Archimedean point on which to stand and from which to act, in the very uncertain and ambiguous processes of nature and history.

I see in this perspective the magna charta of a truly radical humanism. It is radical because the dignity of human beings is not in what they *have*, in the sum total of their possessions or merits. Their dignity is not in what they *do*, in the list of their conquests and achievements. It is not even in what they *are*, in their personality and character. All these features may be important; all may be genuine expressions of human dignity. However, our ultimate possibility is to be more than we have, do and are: to be and remain the children of our Father, the heirs to God's promise. In this perspective, every human being stands in his or her ultimate human right. No other standards and measures can pass the last judgment about our humanity.

And this is a matter of practical importance. How often human beings are measured by arbitrary standards of the established society and culture! How often are they treated as objects of evaluation and manipulation in politics, production, science and even personal relations! In such an atmosphere, the biblical vision represents initiative for an *unconditional humanism*. It breaks through all the conditions of being human, to find in them and behind them the true dignity of every human child: our own inalienable right founded in our being in the "mind of God", irrespective of what we have or do or are.

There is a practical aspect to this vision of humanity. If the ultimate dignity of the human person is his or her being in the "mind of God" then the "place in this mind" defines the "place for Prometheus". It does so not only with respect to God but also with respect to the rest of *creation*. The "mind of God" is God's creating, sustaining, redeeming love. The *dominium terrae* witnessed to in Psalm 8 has to be understood in this setting. The mandate of this "dominium" (lordship) is then by no means the mandate for arbitrary domination and manipulation. Within the context of the covenant this dominium is to be understood and practised only as a *ministerium terrae*. Without this condition the Promethean mission is bound to become tragic and destructive. The ecological developments in our industrial societies provide a vivid illustration of this.

So far, this lesson has not been taken sufficiently seriously in Christian-Marxist dialogue. The criticism of biological humanists with respect to this failure is justified. Should not *Prometheus* be joined by *Atlas*, the "burden bearer"? To face this challenge and to respond to it might well delineate a "new frontier" for our Christian-Marxist encounters and for ecumenical theology.

NOTES

[1] *Differenz der demokritischen und epikureischen Naturphilosophie* (1840), in *MEGA* I/1, Frankfurt/M, 1927, p.10.

[2] Cf. my book *Christus oder Prometheus? Die Kernfrage des christlich-marxistischen Dialogs und die Christologie*, Hamburg, Furche-Verlag, 1972.

[3] Quoted in Roger Garaudy and Quinton Lauer, *A Christian-Communist Dialogue*, Garden City, Doubleday, 1968, p.54.

[4] *Ibid.*

[5] Ernst Bloch, *Das Prinzip Hoffnung*, III, Berlin, Aufbau Verlag, 1959, p.316.

[6] *Buh není zcela mrtev*, Prague, 1967, p.9.

[7] *Atheismus im Christentum*, Frankfurt/M., Suhrkamp, 1968, p.16.

[8] "Zur Kritik der Hegelschen Rechtsphilosophie, Einleitung" (1844), in Karl Marx, *Die Frühschriften* ed. S. Landshut, Stuttgart, Kröner, 1953, p.216.

4.

The Unnecessary God?
The Idea of God
and the Quest for Human Identity

In January 1967 I had a memorable encounter with a leading German theologian in my apartment in Prague. Jürgen Moltmann brought me a copy of *Time* magazine and drew my attention to the cover story about the recent developments in American theology. The title of the article was "God is dead". I was somehow perplexed by that piece of information coming from "God's own country". However, I was able to present my friend with a series of articles which had just appeared in a leading literary magazine in my own country. By that time, Czechoslovakia had already been twenty years under the pressures of official aetheistic indoctrination. Therefore, for many in West and East it figured as a firmly established stronghold of atheism. Yet the title of the Czech series was: "God is not quite dead".

This incident sounded an early warning to me at a time when I was invited to teach in the West, at the Union Theological Seminary in New York City and at the University of Basel. The warning was soon confirmed by first experiences. The theme of God seemed to have dropped out of the major trends of Western theology. Especially during my first years in Switzerland, I encountered groups of theological students who were much more interested in social problems than in fundamental theological issues. My lectures on Marxism attracted them more than those on dogmatics. The social interest pleased me. The neglect of theology annoyed me. An unexpected challenge had to be faced: the very central theme of theology, the question of God, recently rediscovered among some Marxists in the East, had to be restated among some theologians in the West.

How to respond to such a challenge? In what sense is the idea of God theologically and anthropologically necessary? Here the issue of identity became particularly urgent, in all its three dimensions: anthropological, theological and ecumenical. One had to reflect on both the central place of the idea of God in classical Christian thought and on the changes of its context in contemporary culture.

Eclipse of the obligatory idea of God

The question of God has become an open theme today both for our culture and theology. It has ceased to be a matter of course. The idea of God has lost its ideologically self-evident character. Dietrich Bonhoeffer was one of the first to draw our attention to these profound changes. From his Berlin cell on 8 June 1944 he wrote to his friend Eberhard Bethge:

> Human beings have learned to deal with themselves in all questions of importance without recourse to the "working hypothesis" called "God". In questions of science, art and ethics, this has become an understood thing at which one now hardly dares to tilt. But for the last hundred years or so it has also become increasingly true of religious questions; it is becoming evident that everything gets along without "God" — and, in fact, just as well as before. As in the scientific field, so in human affairs generally, "God is being pushed more and more out of life, losing more and more ground".[1]

These words have sometimes been misunderstood. They were interpreted, for example, as paving the way for an abandonment of *faith* in God, as a blueprint for an "atheistic theology", or even as encouraging a complete break with theology and as a prelude to the atheism of the future. Bonhoeffer himself, however, was looking in a different direction. His statements were formulated quite consciously *coram Deo* (in God's presence): "God himself compels us to recognize it (this truth)... He compels us to a true acknowledgment of our situation in his presence."[2] How should we understand him?

Bonhoeffer's words reflect the radically *changed context* in which we and our contemporaries confront the question of God. For thousands of years the theme of God was part and parcel of Western thought. "God" was part of the stock-in-trade of the dominant world-view. The sophisticated version of this axiom was the metaphysical theistic concept of God — the great achievement of Western civilization in the philosophical and theological realm. God is the First Principle and the Final Goal, the Guarantor of meaning and the ultimate Arbiter of our human life.

> In theistic metaphysics, the Deity was the necessary basis for the continued existence and concept of reality as a whole and in all its parts, a basis which is inescapable for human thought and on which in the last analysis everything finite and incapable of independent existence rests and is sustained in being; and all this is so in the best and most beneficial sense for the whole universe.[3]

The interests of philosophical theory, practical morality, and organized religion (not to mention politics and culture) coalesced to produce the logical conclusion: *God exists.* Even in the case of theology and the church, the almost axiomatic presupposition of thought and action was to a large extent the framework of the theistic metaphysical world-view inspired by that overall vision.

Bonhoeffer considers the shaking and even the possible collapse of this theistic world-view, and particularly the consequent loss of the quasi-axiomatic character of the theme of God. He points to the historical and sociological developments in modern culture that are usually described and analyzed in terms of *secularization.*[4] He ventures a prognosis which, after more than four decades, now stands in need of certain modifications. Nevertheless, he seems to be fundamentally right. In our culture, the axiomatic character of the idea of God seems to have disappeared.

What does this fundamental insight imply? A "final solution" to the question of God? The death of God? This is in fact the conclusion reached by certain of our contemporaries. For a while, even the theologians seemed to lose their head. "Death of God theologies" became fashionable. But theologians quickly pulled themselves together. The fact that the theme of God had lost its self-evident character, guaranteed by the dominant ideology, did not automatically mean, they soon realized, that this theme had to bow out. They were helped by the reference to the *sources.* Certainly the God of the prophets and apostles was no self-evident God who could be taken for granted. Quite the reverse! Experience of God as attested in the Bible is inseparable from an atmosphere of surprise, amazement, dread and, above all, joy. This is the case in the Old Testament and even more so in the New Testament. The God of the apostles and prophets is not a predictable, calculable, manipulable God. Far from being a programmed "computer God", a *Dieu machine,* God is the living Spirit, humanity's personal counterpart, our covenant partner free in grace and mercy towards us.

What is attested in the Bible, therefore, is not so much the *concept* of God but rather the *name* of God. The name of this God is Yahweh, the Lord — and the unobvious, not-self-evident character of this biblical God is very impressively reflected in the explanation given of the divine name: I AM WHO I AM (Ex. 3:14) or, closer to the original Hebrew: I WILL BE WHO I WILL BE. The God who speaks here is not a God of *necessity* but rather the God of *freedom.*

In his major work entitled "God as Mystery of the World", published in 1977, Eberhard Jüngel, a Protestant theologian who has devoted himself particularly to the contemporary question of God in the light of the changes in the intellectual and cultural climate of modern times, formulates his conclusion in the lapidary thesis: God is not necessary. "God is more than necessary."[5] I find this formula helpful.

God is not necessary. We say goodbye here to the obvious, self-evident God; to the God who is built into our dominant world-view and forms part and parcel of it; to the proofs of God's existence if these proofs are regarded as more than faith's intelligent attempts to understand and explain itself, i.e. to the extent that these proofs seek to help with the recognition of God, to demonstrate by a Herculean intellectual effort the necessity of God's existence. But we also say goodbye here — and this is an essential, practical, cultural and socio-political consequence — to the *obligatory, compulsory God* whom believers impose on their fellow human beings, over-riding their minds and consciences and even threatening sanctions in case of non-conformity. We must say goodbye to such a God — and do so not simply under the pressures of a new historical era but because we are led to do so by fresh reflection on the source of our faith. For such a God is not the God of faith. The God of faith is different — He is *not* necessary.

God is more than necessary. Freedom is the counterpoint and correlate of necessity. It seems to me most significant, in fact, that the *Sitz im Leben* (life setting) of the disclosure, the revelation of the biblical name of God is the account of the liberation of the people of God. In the Old Testament, for example, the context is the history of the Exodus, the event in which Israel experiences its deliverance from bondage. In the New Testament, the fundamental context is the Easter story of Jesus. One of the most pregnant "definitions" of God is found in Paul's letter to the Romans (4:24). He is the God "who raised Jesus from the dead". In other words, here again God's name is proclaimed in the context of the supreme human need for freedom, freedom from our last enemy, temporal and eternal death. "In the Bible, God is... centrally identified with a promise of life, with an incursion of life into the world of death."[6]

The name of God is connected with this concrete, humanly essential content, with the grounding and promise of freedom in the world of necessities. We human beings are in some respects "creatures of necessity". We are dependent on nature, limited and determined by our own psychological and physical constitution, entangled in complex cultural and historical contexts, conditioned by structures and indeed by material pressures of our economic and social destiny. Karl Marx put his finger on something fundamental when he declared succinctly: "The human being — that is the world of the human being." "The human essence is the ensemble of social relations."[7] No realistic anthropology can possibly ignore the relative truth of these statements; not even theology can ignore it, theology least of all, if it does not want to remain within the realm of the arbitrary and the idealistic.

But for all its recognition of the importance of this dimension of necessity, the reference to the divine name establishes at the same time the counterpoint: the human being is not simply the *world* of the human being. The human being cannot be explained completely in terms of "the ensemble of social relations". In the concrete language of the Bible, the human person, this child of necessity taken from the dust of the earth, has been made in the likeness of God and is therefore the child of freedom, in the midst of necessities related to what is "more than necessary". Jesus states this truth in the simple axiom: "Humanity lives not by bread alone but by every word that proceeds from the mouth of God" (Matt. 4:4). In this utterance of biblical wisdom, the importance of daily bread is in no sense minimized. Bread — and in modern terms this means its production and distribution, i.e. an efficient economy and participatory social system — has its honoured place in God's sight. It is not for nothing that "daily bread" has its place in the Lord's prayer, the model of all calling upon God. But the fact remains: the human being cannot live in a truly human way by bread *alone* — not even in the most energetic search for an efficient and just system of production and distribution. Bread is necessary: the Word is more than necessary. The Word, the truth of the Word, transforms creatures of necessity into children of freedom.

To avoid any possible misunderstanding here, I would emphasize that what I am stating is not that the dignity of the human being is simply coextensive with the sphere of the "more than necessary". The dignity of the human being is already at stake in "the question of bread", in the conditions of daily life and work. But the reminder of this sphere of the "more than necessary" enables us to pose the question of human dignity in a truly radical way, to focus it on the inalienable personal core. It makes quite clear that the human being can never be fully accounted for in terms of what is necessary, plannable and feasible. Significant though the criteria of production and performance may be in their place, they do not suffice to determine the value of the human person. This truth shows us the direction to be taken in the indispensable efforts to achieve, for example, a genuine "humanization of the world of labour" or to create a more humane social and political order. Conditioned though the human person may be in every respect, he/she has been given an *unconditional* dignity.

In the cultural and intellectual tradition of the West, the reference to God served to undergird this incalculable dignity of humanity, this unconditional human right and claim. To be sure, this reference to God does not stand here in splendid isolation; it is not only theology which ensures that the dimension of the "more than necessary" is taken seriously; in their own way, philosophy, art and even science, also help in this direction. Nor is the case that the reference to God automatically and infallibly serves this end; in the hands of cynical hypocrites and in the failures of believers, this reference to God can be misused in a manner inimical to humanity. Here, too, the dimension of the non-self-evident in the theme of God must be borne in mind. I am firmly convinced, however, that, in spite of everything, unquenchable impulses for freedom are latent in the biblical understanding of God and that these impulses can be helpfully transmitted even in our world today.

The liberating power of the remembrance of God
I venture to speak of this conviction not simply as a dogmatic position but also as something which I have *experienced* in my own life, particularly as a Christian who has spent a considerable portion of his days in Eastern Europe. This region of the world is particularly relevant in the present context because East European culture and society have been for decades, in the era of the established Marxist socialism, the scene of a complex and aggressive effort "to settle the religious question" in a radically atheistic way, by erasing the theme of God from the annals of human history. The motives behind this attempt were varied. There were not only the traditional atheistic components of historical and dialectical materialism but also the determination of the Communist Party — inspired by ideology and the power-political lust — to secure complete control over the souls of its fellow-citizens. Belief in God, the ideologues rightly sensed, was an obstacle to this complete control. From the standpoint of the official claim to cultural and political monopoly it represented a "random factor" which therefore had to be eliminated as far as possible.

As I see it, we are mistaken to regard these atheistic efforts simply as a non-success or failure. For one thing, the time so far accorded them — i.e. the forty to seventy years of Marxist experiments in Eastern Europe — is too short to permit an assessment. Nor is it possible to ignore certain successes registered by this anti-religious cultural policy. In the East

European countries, with the exception of Poland, religion has in fact receded to quite a considerable extent, at least as far as official cultural life is concerned.

However, this recession of religion is surely only one side of the coin. One of my most vivid human and theological experiences in Czechoslovakia was the discovery that this process was far from being a straightforward one-dimensional business but was rather an intensely dialectic and two-sided one. Far from vanishing from the range of vital human interests, this officially silenced theme of God became for some, for the first time, in the very midst of attempts to suppress it officially, an even more "question-able" theme in both senses of this word, i.e. a real question, an open question, and also one which was worthy of being asked, an explosive question, a supremely relevant human theme. Indeed, at the very moment when it lost the official protection of society, just when it became culturally displaced and "homeless" in virtue of the shattering of all its internal and external ideological self-evidence, the theme of God took on fresh actuality and credibility.

It was no accident that the fresh relevance of the question of God should have become transparent in the course of the Christian-Marxist dialogue in the sixties, even for the Marxists involved. This became evident in two respects in particular: in the context of the quest for a solid basis for personal identity in face of both life and death; and in the question as to how the established system, dogmatically fetishized, could be broken open to let in fresh air, i.e. the question of a transcendence permitting the dawn of more humane possibilities in social life. Precisely on the crusty surface of the Stalinist system, the inexhaustible relevance of the theme of God was demonstrated both for the individual and for society.

In the question of identity, the reference to God offered a refreshing alternative in at least two respects: it helped to clarify the fact (1) that personal human existence could not be totally controlled, and (2) that this existence was set within a radically open horizon.

1. The former emphasis demonstrated its relevance, above all, in face of the totalitarian claims of the dominant ideology. This official ideology and its power structures sought to persuade citizens that the question of the meaning of life was best left to the supreme authorities of the "realized socialist society" and to its Party; they could safely leave this question in their official hands: "Trust the Party, comrades!" — people were urged, exactly in moments when this "faith in Party" was becoming increasingly

dubious to so many thoughtful people — for example, in face of the manipulated political show-trials of the fifties.

In face of the answers officially proposed, the remembrance of God kept the questions alive: Is it really possible for me to delegate the question of my identity, the identity of my human existence, my knowledge, my conscience, to some ideology or political party? Does this question not arise in a context which simply cannot be decreed or controlled by other human beings and even less by institutions? Does not our human existence have an inalienable reference and dimension in which we are permitted and commanded to live out our human destiny in personal identity — each one of us individually in his or her irreplaceable responsibility?

2. Inseparable from this is the other free space which, in a materialistically planned (or practised) society in particular, the remembrance of God keeps open for us. The memory of God frames the questions about our identity in a radically open horizon. In our quest for a life of genuine identity and authenticity, there *is* a further beyond — a *plus ultra*. There is *hope* of identity and, indeed, even in view of the "last enemy", death. As we have already seen, the reference to God — the name of God — points not only to the dimension of depth in understanding earthly human existence but also to its hope in time and in eternity. The question of identity is thereby placed in an eschatological horizon. "It does not yet appear what we shall be" (1 John 3:2) — the New Testament text the Marxist philosopher Ernst Bloch was so fond of quoting — is to be taken to heart over and over again. It is the promise that the hope of identity transcends our achievements and our failures.

That the importance of the theme of God for the question of identity should have been sensed so powerfully in an atheistic culture in face of death in particular should not surprise us. I recall the funeral services (these were, by the way, practically the only possibility the churches had of addressing non-churchgoing fellow citizens directly). These services became a supremely important opportunity of witness — recognized even by many "outsiders", with hesitation perhaps, with wonder, yet with intense interest. For many people, even "practising atheists", an alternative was offered here, a question-able yet at the same time credible alternative.

Testimony of a captive

I conclude this chapter with a literary reference. One of the most impressive and credible reflections on the theme of identity I have read recently is by Vaclav Havel, a well-known Czech playwright. Until recently, he was kept in prison in Czechsolovakia. He was allowed to write very little in the prison, not much more than rather short letters to his wife. However, during the course of 1982 he used this modest opportunity to compose in sequel form his philosophical-theological reflections. From them resulted an impressive essay on elementary questions of human destiny in today's world. In the centre lies the theme: *identity*.

Like many contemporary writers and thinkers, Havel has suffered from the spiritual and human misery of our time, i.e. from the threat to personal human existence through alienating pressures of ideological and power-political machinery as well as through manipulative mechanisms of our technocratically oriented civilization. He sees the deepest origins of these tragic occurrences in the "crisis in the experience of the absolute horizon".

Wherever this horizon fades or is barred, there human beings only too easily become incapacitated victims of such pressures. "Only a human being can lead a relatively tolerable life in this world, which is oriented 'beyond' this world; a human being, who refers to the infinite, the absolute and the eternal with every one of his or her 'here's' and every one of his or her 'now's'. An unconditional orientation upon 'now' and 'here' converts every bearable 'now' and 'here' into desert and wilderness and finally discolours it with blood."[8]

For our search for identity, therefore, the awakening to the transcendent dimension of human life — the metaphysical and theological question — is of fundamental significance. The hope for identity grows with it and, in addition, the prospect for meaningful engagement in our workaday world:

> If I adhere to that which the world makes out of me — namely a little screw belonging to a gigantic machine, which robs me of my human identity — then I cannot do much... However, if I think about what each one of us originally is, or what he or she — independent of the world situation — could potentially become, namely, a human being of full age, I can obviously do much. For example, I can try to behave in a way that appears to be proper to me and in a way all persons should conduct themselves according to my deepest conviction— namely in full responsibility. Upon the objection that it makes no sense, I would quite simply answer: "Oh yes! It does make sense!"[9]

NOTES

[1] *Letters and Papers from Prison*, London, SCM Press, 1971, pp.325f.

[2] *Ibid*, p.360.

[3] H.G. Geyer, "Atheismus und Christentum", *Evang. Theologie*, 1968, p.266.

[4] Cf. my book *Herrschaft Christi in der säkularisierten Welt*, Zurich, EVZ-Verlag, 1967.

[5] *Gott als Geheimnis der Welt: Zur Begründung der Theologie des Gekreuzigten im Streit zwischen Theismus und Atheismus*, Tübingen, J.C.B. Mohr, 1977, p.30.

[6] Helmut Gollwitzer, *Krummes Holz — aufrechter Gang: Zur Frage nach dem Sinn des Lebens*, München, Chr. Kaiser, 1970, p.284.

[7] Karl Marx, "Thesen über Feuerbach", in *Die Frühschriften*, ed. S. Landshut, Stuttgart, Kröner, 1953, p.340.

[8] Vaclav Havel, *Dopisy Olze*, Toronto, Sixty-eight Publishers, 1985, pp.434f.

[9] *Ibid.*, pp.344f.

5.
Theology in a Pluralistic Society: Zeal for Truth and Tolerance

One of the major challenges for a theologian coming from a Marxist society to teach in the West is the great change in the atmosphere around him. The severe climate of a system, dominated by one official ideology and permanently scrutinized for suspected deviations by administrative measures, is replaced by the milder air of a pluralistic society, tolerating a wide spectrum of choice and opinion.

Such a change is both liberating and bewildering. It is *liberating* to be able not only to think but also to speak and to act without the need to worry about the powerful censor passing judgment on one's ideas. It is also *bewildering:* in the complex pluralism and relativism of the Western "open market of ideas" the scene is dominated by "supplies" of puzzling variety, an incredible "supermarket of possibilities". Anything goes — in cultures and sometimes in the churches. Worse still, theology itself appears unsure of itself, engaging in feverish efforts to make itself more attractive by borrowing from its more fashionable sister-rivals on the marketplace — from psychology, sociology and other allied disciplines. Its identity becomes insecure and indistinct.

In a certain sense it seems to be easier to teach theology in the frosty atmosphere in the East where the issues have a clearer shape and contour than in the somehow foggy spiritual milieu of our Western societies. How are we to respond theologically to such a challenge? This has been the question occupying my mind ever since I came to the West.

I would like to present some reflections on the theme of theology in a pluralistic society under the title "Zeal for Truth and Tolerance". The formulation suggests a thesis: responsible theological engagement in a pluralistic culture presupposes both concern for truth and tolerance. My ecumenical involvement and my academic experiences form the *Sitz im Leben* for such a thesis.

In our response to the challenge of pluralistic society we are threatened from both sides. There is a zeal for truth which violates and destroys tolerance. Everyone knows how many zealous, militant and fanatical exponents of truth have been active in history and still are. There is a murderous zeal for truth, which insists on "truth" at all costs — *fiat veritas pereat mundus!* — an excluding, excommunicating zeal, which has so often been displayed even by Christian theologians (and, of course, by ardent atheistic ideologues too).

But on the other side there is a tolerance which shies away from any reference whatever to truth, a type of human behaviour characterizing those who no longer believe anything themselves and therefore find it easy to be tolerant. We find examples of this, too, in history past and present, in the camp of the sceptics and radical relativists and even nihilists. Here there is a refusal to engage in the quest for the truth; binding decisions and commitments are avoided on principle. Here any zeal for truth displayed by others is greeted with pained resignation or, worse still, with a cynical smile and the familiar counter-question: what is truth?

It is perhaps here, in this controversial area so packed with tensions for church, culture and society, that we are confronted with one of the most critical challenges of our time. Both for the spirit of our theological ministry and for the spiritual health of civilization itself, the responses we make to this challenge are of considerable importance.

Salvation in no one else

The zeal for truth is deeply rooted in our Jewish and Christian tradition. The Czech Reformer, Jan Hus, expressed the basic commitment of Christian faith and life in the following summons: "Faithful Christian, search for truth, hear the truth, learn the truth, hold the truth, defend the truth until death."[1] Hus was faithful to the central emphasis of the biblical message. The zealous concern for truth is a fundamental element and motivation of the prophetic and apostolic witness.

The message and ministry of the prophets of Israel, so vividly exemplified in the life of a Moses, the struggle of an Elijah, or the sufferings of a Jeremiah, was surely this: zeal for the honour, the name, the truth of Yahweh! However diverse the individual prophets and their destinies, the one common denominator in every case is surely this active zeal for Yahweh's glory, for Yahweh's incomparable Name, for the incontestable claim of God's truth. This comes out with blazing clarity in the supreme affirmations of Israel's faith: in the *Shema Israel*, for example, or the first commandment of the Decalogue: "Hear, O Israel! The Lord our God is one Lord. Thou shalt love the Lord thy God with all thy heart, with all thy soul, and with all thy strength!" (Deut. 6:4f.). "Thou shalt have no other gods beside Me!" (Ex. 20:3). Here, in this exclusive and all-inclusive devotion to the one God, Yahweh, to the one God for whom there are no substitutes, is the root and source of the prophets' zeal for truth.

The zeal for truth of the New Testament apostles also has its roots and source in the prophetic fire. The *feu sacré* — the sacred flame — of Easter and Pentecost propels them forward in an eschatologically accelerated movement out "into all the world". This becomes particularly evident in the case of Paul, unquestionably the most zealous of all the apostles. But his is no indiscriminate zeal. From his own personal experience as a former persecutor, he knew only too well that there is such a thing as a mistaken zeal (Phil. 3:6). It is no accident that "zeal" (in the sense of blind passion) occurs in the apostle's catalogue of vices (Gal. 5:20). Clearly, there is such a thing as an "unenlightened" zeal for God, a "zeal without knowledge" (Rom. 10:2), and Paul warns his fellow Christians against it. This warning must be borne in mind. The criterion which determines the legitimacy of our zeal for truth is not its intensity, not the temperature of a zealous temperament, but the element of truth itself. In this element legitimate zeal prospers and is to be developed and displayed.

To understand more fully what this means, let us turn to a central New Testament expression of this zeal for truth, an axiomatic statement which is also open to misunderstanding: "There is salvation in no one else" (Acts 4:12). This pithy statement is found in one of the first Christian sermons (presented in the usual stylized literary form in Acts), in which Peter explains why, despite explicit prohibition and the risk of persecution, the apostles are unable to give up confessing their faith in the crucified and risen Jesus Christ.

The sentence quoted is no fortuitous one but reflects a recurring emphasis of the New Testament message. Although the New Testament witness is a complex one borne by a mixed chorus of voices whose underlying harmony it is not always easy to discern, there is a constant *cantus firmus* audible in this polyphony, namely, its attestation of the unique and radical importance of the life and history of the man from Nazareth. John states it as follows: "Grace and truth came through Jesus Christ" (John 1:17). Paul testifies to this basic conviction by affirming: "No other foundation can anyone lay than that which has been laid, which is Jesus Christ" (1 Cor. 3:11). And Peter, continuing the statement we have quoted, avers: "For there is no other name under heaven given among men by which we must be saved" (Acts 4:12).

This is a remarkable unanimity — as well as a prodigious claim to truth. It is not just to our pluralistically attuned ears that this sounds like a "tall order"; it already came as something of a shock to the people in the apostles' audiences. When primitive Christianity appeared on the stage of Hellenistic religious history, people were confronted with a movement which adopted a very different strategy from that of the prevailing religious syncretism. When the early Christian missionaries turned up in the various Aeropagi near and far in their society, they were, of course, quite ready to be "Jews to the Jews and Greeks to the Greeks" (1 Cor. 9:20), ready to enter sympathetically into the specific cultural and intellectual situation of their fellow human beings, but this never implied any readiness to treat the name and truth of Jesus Christ as in any sense relative and exchangeable.

The result was a provocative breach of the generally accepted rules of the bewilderingly exuberant "market in possible religions" with its mutual trading in salvation and saviours. In their zeal for truth, Christians insisted on the clear and historically concrete contours of the truth they attested. The salvation they proclaimed had a quite distinct profile, the human face of Jesus of Nazareth. To most of their religious contemporaries, this seemed like unfair competition, and even evidence of religious crudity and naivety. Under the pressure of this "public opinion", indeed, attempts would soon be made even in the church itself to soften this "hard line" and to reach compromises. The apostolic message proved extremely unwilling, however, to yield to syncretistic temptations. "There is salvation in no one else; for there is no other name... by which we must be saved."

The key in our present context is this: Are we to interpret this powerful emphasis as an intolerant claim to absoluteness and exclusivity? Was it here that the tracks were irrevocably fixed leading eventually, with iron necessity, to the syndromes of fanaticism and intolerance which later marred the course of Christianity in history? The fact that some historians and philosophers incline to this conclusion makes us pause for reflection. Several considerations, however, warn us against accepting their arguments too easily. If we are to track the specific apostolic zeal for truth down to its source, a more concrete and detailed examination of the biblical context of this short axiomatic statement is called for. What inspires it is no narrow spirit of opinionated exclusiveness but a spirit of a very different kind. Three points at least seem to be worth making.

1. *There is salvation in no one else.* This statement has a quite clear and specific reference, not to some anonymous or even arbitrary subject but, on the contrary, to a quite definite subject, to a specifically named person: Jesus Christ. What is set forth here is not an abstract doctrine of the absolute. It is faith which is attested here, faith in Jesus the Lord; faith, moreover, in Jesus Christ alone, not faith, for example, in Christians or Christianity. This is not a statement about the "absoluteness of Christianity". The attempts so often made under this rubric in modern religious philosophy and theology, with a view to demonstrating the superiority of Christianity over all other religions, is basically of no interest to the New Testament writers. The apostles preach not themselves, not the wealth of their own ideas or their own radiant virtues, but exclusively "Christ and him crucified" (1 Cor. 1:23). This is quite crucial and must be taken with the utmost seriousness: in the light precisely of the cross, all human claims — even and especially all Christian claims — are radically "crossed out". If Christians should nevertheless persist in parading them, even *ad maiorem ecclesiae gloriam* — for the greater glory of the church, then shades of a spiritual schizophrenia become visible; they are a living contradiction of the real basis of their faith.

2. *There is salvation in no one else.* This statement refers not only to a specifically named person but also to the history inseparable from that name: the history of Jesus of Nazareth. It is given its substantial content by this history. It is not an empty statement (or claim) which can be arbitrarily assigned content but one which has already been given its own obligatory profile. Its direction and thrust are indicated by the history of Jesus, and this has an unmistakable central characteristic — namely, Jesus' devotion to his fellow human beings in their manifold need. This is no nebulous devotion but a sharply profiled one of partisanship and identification with those who are pushed to the edge of society, its outcasts, "the weary and heavy-laden" (Matt. 11:28). But precisely in this "bias", in this "preferential option for the poor", it is not exclusive; rather it is a bold move towards fellow human beings transcending all barriers and prejudices. It is *this* history (and not any other) which the evangelists and prophets interpret as "God's exodus to humanity", to the near and the far. And they follow him in their mission, in a welcoming, inclusive movement, not a dismissive, excluding one, for in Jesus Christ "there is neither Jew nor Greek, neither slave nor free, neither male nor female" (Gal. 3:28). When the primitive Christian community proclaims that "there is salvation in no one else", it is to this definite history which crosses all frontiers that it is bearing witness. The implication of this,

however, is that the clear-cut confession of Christ and his way, far from building any barriers between human beings, radically challenges all such barriers. The "exclusive" starting point of the Christian faith inaugurates an "inclusive" history".[2]

3. *There is salvation in no one else.* In the name and history of Jesus Christ, what is at stake is salvation. In other words, we are confronted here not just with something neutral and ambivalent, nor even with a combination of both "Yes" and "No" (still less with a hybrid "Yesno"!), but with God's "Yes" to us all. In what way is witness to be borne to such salvation? In a way which would suggest that this salvation is a special privilege of us Christians? That hardly chimes with the history of Christ himself. On the contrary, we are to bear witness to this salvation as a summons of faith, as an invitation to our fellow human beings to "climb aboard" the salvation history, to join in passing on this "good news for all" to our fellow human beings. For it is "good news", not an ambiguous message. The Greek New Testament knows the *eu*angelion — the gospel — not a *dys*angelion, a message of doom. This is an offer of grace, and both terms here must be given their full value. It is an offer — urgent, certainly, but no impersonal Diktat; and it is an offer of grace — certainly not cheap, undemanding grace, yet not over-riding compulsion either. It was a wicked mistake when the church, after it had become powerful, legitimized its evangelistic practice of compulsory conversion by an appeal to, of all things, the generously welcoming parable of the "Great Banquet" (Luke 14:15-24) in which, with a refreshing absence of prejudice and disregard for deeply anchored conventions, Jesus shows his particular concern for the "outsiders". It was a sinful misunderstanding if the only point the church noticed in this parable — and even this on the basis of a mistranslation — was the *compelle intrare* (compel them to come in)! Far from being in any sense authorized by the primitive Christian confession of faith, such a strategy is a complete contradiction of it.

What are the implications of these three points for our theme "zeal for truth and tolerance"? In the first place, they give the lie to the assumption that the unambiguous New Testament confession of Christ is bound logically to lead to intolerant behaviour. If we take seriously what this confession says, and especially its naming of Jesus Christ, it points in quite a different direction, namely, towards co-humanity in solidarity.

But Christian theologians are well-advised not to insist too emphatically and self-confidently on this repudiation. The gales of church history blow in our faces telling us that the facts are against us in this respect! We cannot and should not deny that it was possible for an unambiguous confession of Christ to develop in the direction of a mistaken exclusivity, a claim to monopoly, arrogance, into aggression and inquisition. *Vestigia terrent* — the footprints frighten us because they lead to our own door. In the house of the church and theology there is still much cleaning up to be done in the matter of tolerance. But the obligation to learn from the mistakes of the past does not require us to abandon the biblical zeal for truth. We must not throw away the baby — the Christmas baby — with the bath-water. As the three points just made have shown, there is no inevitable direct connection between the confession of Christ and intolerance.

In the light of the confession of Christ, however, is that all we can say on the theme of "zeal for truth and tolerance"? Do we have to be content with this somewhat qualified and defensive answer that there is no inevitable connection between this faith and intolerance? Or can the argument be taken further and this provisional answer be developed in a positive way? In other words, can we move in the direction of a mutually enriching convergence between the two poles in this field of tension? I am persuaded that this is possible. Which brings me to the second stage in the argument of this essay, in which attention will be focused primarily on the theme of tolerance.

Tolerance and indifference

The development of the concept and reality of tolerance in the history of civilization and in contemporary practice is a complex one. Tolerance "can be taken to cover the whole range of graduations, from the mere recognition of freedom of conscience (provided the dissenter keeps his opinions to himself and does not publicize them), to the higher stage where the right to practise religion first privately and then to hold public services is guaranteed, up to the highest level of all, where all religions dissenting from that which originally had exclusive rights are freely permitted."[3] The several stages form a coherent movement and merge into one another, because the history of tolerance is a dynamic one with a built-in momentum in the direction of "higher stages", though, of course, with frequent relapses.

The complexity of the reality of tolerance itself is matched by the complexity of its underlying motivation. In the history of toleration in the West, a variety of impulses were operative. The Toleration Edict of Joseph II[4] reminds us of the considerable contribution made by the rationalism of the Enlightenment: the conviction that there is only one rational human nature common to all human beings makes it possible not merely to tolerate but even to respect its diverse historical expressions in religions and cultures. Even earlier, of course, the humanists of the Reformation period worked for toleration. There is the work of an Erasmus or a Castellio,[5] for example, who were led in this same direction both by the tradition of antiquity and the spirit of the gospel, away from fanaticism of every kind and towards tolerance. Nor can we ignore the heartening contribution of such patently Christian thinkers as Jan Amos Comenius, who, despite serious opposition close to home, brought into prominence once again basic elements in the biblical faith which are favourable to tolerance, such as the biblical emphasis on the supremacy of God's truth and grace over all human judgments; and the recognition that our zeal for truth can only find authentic expression in that loving solidarity with our fellow human beings which we find concretely embodied in the life and teaching of Jesus of Nazareth. Nor should the reminder of these impulses blind us to the fact that the history of toleration not only had its intellectual and spiritual motivation but also its only too solid economic and political dimension. The French jurist and man of letters, Etienne Pasquier, wittily summed up the bitter experience of this latter dimension in his couplet of 1570:

> Qui voudra Réunir avec Ruiner
>   mettre
> Il verra qu'il n'y a transport que
>   d'une lettre![6]

In other words, an intolerant and dictatorial religious policy leads to economic ruin.

There is no call to play up any of these different motivations to tolerance at the expense of the others. Each in its own way helped to ward off the dangers of fanaticism and intolerance in human society.

The same is also true even of the moods of weariness at the unanswerable question of truth and of the tendencies to a scepticism and relativism which sometimes end up in an attitude of utter indifference. Yet this ambiguous diversity of motivation makes delimitation necessary. From the theological standpoint, at any rate, we must affirm quite categorically that tolerance in the Christian sense can never be equated with indifference. Not only because zeal for truth and the Christian confession demand decision in the matter of truth, but also because the command to love God and our neighbour excludes relationships of sheer indifference. Love courts fellow human beings, sides with them, and therefore struggles with them for the truth.

As the Christian understands it, therefore, tolerance does not mean a non-committal laissez-faire attitude of indulgence. It is not *indifferentia* (indifference) but rather a transaction *in differentia* (in the difference); in other words, a transaction in which differences are mutually related and patiently borne with. As Gollwitzer says: "In its broadest sense, tolerance is patience with the other human being in his or her difference."[7] Understood in this way, therefore, to be tolerant does not mean making light of tensions and hushing them up in a relativistic way, as if the question of truth were of no real consequence at all. In the words of a Quaker and pacifist: "Tolerance is the battlefield on which the struggle for truth is to be waged."[8]

But is it really possible in practice to stick to this conception of tolerance with all its inherent tensions? Do not the demons of intolerance which we are trying to exorcise here once again spring to life? There is no denying this danger. Further clarification is required. A reminiscence from the field of biblical theology may help us a little.

There is nuanced discussion of our theme in Rudolf Bultmann's commentary on John's Gospel, precisely at the point, moreover, where Bultmann seeks to interpret the important Johannine "I am", one of the most emphatic passages in the New Testament witness to Christ and truth.

> The *ego eimi* of Jesus always means that there is only *one* leader to salvation, only *one* revealer. In the matter of salvation there is only the one possibility, not many different possibilities. A decision is demanded. Herein lies the intolerance of revelation... It is, of course, the revelation which is intolerant. Human beings can only be tolerant to each other, and, to the degree they are called to represent the intolerant claim of revelation, this claim is directed first and foremost against themselves. When the *homo religiosus* and the dogmatician are intolerant, it is not the intolerance of revelation.[9]

Formulated in such general terms, Bultmann's statements are to some extent open to misunderstanding. A more concrete formulation would bring out the fact that what we have here is not a general ideology of revelation but a witness to Christ. Taken in this sense, Bultmann's main distinction seems to me a most important one. Tolerance towards fellow human beings does not exclude a serious and binding decision of faith and belief (and, in this sense, "intolerance" in the matter of truth, or, better still, zeal for truth), nor, conversely, does such a decision of faith exclude tolerance towards the fellow human being. Where this distinction is not made, where tolerance towards the fellow human being leads us to relativize the question of truth, or where, on the contrary, the zeal of our commitment to truth is prolonged to include intolerance towards our neighbour, then the biblical understanding both of truth and tolerance is distorted and misrepresented. Only in the tension between unconditional obligation to the truth known and confessed, and a sympathetic receptivity to and solidarity with those who think differently — who surely "stand or fall" to their own Lord (and not to us!) — can we be faithful to the witness to Christ.

Two fronts struggle

The effort to define responsibly the relation between zeal for "truth" and "tolerance" in the light of the biblical witness, therefore, is always a struggle on two fronts. It is a struggle, on the one hand, against the temptation to employ coercive and dictatorial means in order to make the witness to truth (even with the best of intentions and in the service of the most benign ends) and, on the other hand, against the temptation to interpret and practise toleration as if it dispensed us individually and socially from decision and commitment in the matter of truth and, if we are Christians, in witness to Christ as the truth. Stated positively, zeal for truth and tolerance go together. They can and should be mutually related. We have to live with, respect, and work creatively with the tension inherent in our theme; and do so in order to safeguard both terms from misinterpretation and misuse. For, to paraphrase a dictum of Immanuel Kant's, without tolerance, zeal for truth is blind: without zeal for truth, tolerance is empty.

Blind zeal and spiritual emptiness — these are the two sicknesses which, if not "unto death" (Kierkegaard), are certainly conditions serious and critical enough to endanger human life — individual and social — even and perhaps especially in affluent societies. Latently, of course, these two dangers are present in every individual and social situation. Depending on the particular circumstances, however, one or the other danger may, of course, predominate and represent the greater temptation. Am I mistaken in feeling that it is the struggle on the second front which is especially relevant today in the climate and conditions prevailing in Western pluralistic society — in the Swiss church and society, for example — the struggle against the temptation to think of tolerance as exempting us from decision and commitment in the matter of truth?

I do not minimize the first of these two dangers, that of individual and collective intolerance. How could I possibly do so in view of my first-hand experience over many years of conditions in which civil and religious liberty was under constant threat — one had to wrestle day in and day out with an ideology and power politics which used all conceivable means to establish its "truth" by intimidating and excluding other options? Even in the West, it is impossible for me to ignore tendencies towards intolerance, though here, of course, such tendencies are very diffuse in character. There are the temptations born of a militant and self-righteous mentality and strategy even in our churches, particularly, though not exclusively, on the extreme right wing of the theological and political spectrum. Such tendencies and temptations have to be opposed and counteracted.

However, if we think of the spiritual climate in our academic communities, is not the insidious growth of indifference in religious, ethical, and political matters an even more acute danger? A pluralism which is not just the acceptance of a legitimate plurality of views in an open society but an ideology of non-commitment, a world-view founded on the renunciation of decision and involvement. A permissiveness which not only advocates greater sympathy for non-conformist life-styles (in itself a perfectly legitimate position) but one which also questions every norm and obligation. A freedom interested mainly in negation, in demolishing restrictions and limitations, a freedom which neglects the positive fulfil-ment of our obligations towards our fellow human beings and is therefore in danger of disappearing in a bottomless void. Do these not constitute symptoms of a wasting disease in the life of society and the church, inevitably provoking people — especially young people — who are looking for meaning to their lives through a passionate protest and desperate attempts to give meaning to political and religious life?

None of the points just made is to be taken as a blanket condemnation but rather as an account of experience. Perhaps, too, as an indication of the reason why, for some of those coming from Eastern Europe, the transition to the West is not only a liberating experience (this it certainly is above all and in spite of everything!) but also, to some extent, a depressing one, especially for those concerned for truly Christian freedom.

Here, I believe, is the context of the special task of theology and of the church. In one of the later volumes of his *Church Dogmatics* Karl Barth wrote: "An existence with no horizon, contour, or shape, one exposed on all sides and therefore at the mercy of every wind that blows, an existence which is consequently the prey to dissolution and disintegration, is a thing of the past for the Christian. The pride and the misery of boundless opining, thinking, and striving is over and done with."[10] The fact is that freedom in the Christian sense, just because it is the freedom made accessible in the history of Christ, also has to reflect the characteristic features of that history. Since freedom in the case of Jesus is a freedom which springs from non-coercive love, these features of freedom in the Christian sense include non-coercive patient tolerance of and readiness for dialogue even with "difficult" contemporaries. At the same time, however, they also include zeal for truth, efforts to introduce the clearly defined impulses of the good news into the behaviour patterns and conditions of our time.

In my view, few things are more otiose and boring than theologies and theologians, sermons and preachers, who no longer take risks for the truth committed to them but, in conformity to the mood of the time, hide this truth, this "light", "under a bushel", shrouding it in the twilight of relativism. Jesus has an apt formula for this behaviour. He called it "savourless salt" (Matt. 5:13; Luther's translation here is *dummes Salz* — "stupid or rubbishy salt"). But for their fermentation processes, our church and our society need the salt of truth, the salt of Jesus. This salt must not lose its savour through our lukewarmness and laziness.

Remembering the "two Karls"

Let me conclude these thoughts on a personal note. In the academic year 1947-48, I was a foreign student in Basle, Switzerland. This was a memorable year in one of the peak periods of the university there, the beginning of its so-called Carolingian Era — the period of the "two Karls" — Karl Barth and Karl Jaspers. The latter had just begun to teach in Basel. I attended the courses of both teachers diligently and with fascination. It was not long, however, before I felt a certain resultant tension, precisely in terms of our theme: "zeal for truth, and tolerance". Certainly both teachers were exponents of both these terms — each in his own distinctive way and with different emphases. In the teaching of Karl Barth we were introduced to an impressively and comprehensively sustained "Christological concentration", to a movement of thought which emphasized that "if it is to be worthy of the name and to edify the Christian church in the world, Christian doctrine must be, in all its statements, exclusively and consistently, directly or indirectly, doctrine of Jesus Christ as the living Word of God addressed to us".[11]

The intellectual world to which we were introduced by the teaching of Karl Jaspers had quite a different structure. Even here, of course, we were lifted into an argument of faith, a philosophical faith. This faith showed great understanding for fundamental themes of the biblical tradition. Without the Bible, Jaspers told us, we in the West slide back into the void, deprived of our human and philosophical roots. The philosopher's openness to biblical thinking, however, halted at a certain point — where it claimed that "there is salvation in no one else". Again and again, Jaspers reached for strong words to express his opposition at this point: "Both in its motivation and in its consequences, this claim is disastrous for us human beings. We must struggle for the truth and for our souls against this fatal claim."[12]

In subsequent years, living in a Marxist-Leninist society, I had frequent occasion to reflect on these two positions and to test their relative strength in critical situations. Global judgments are to be avoided in either case. I make no secret of the fact that for me personally, as for many of my fellow Christians then, Barth's theology, with its focus on the liberating heart of the gospel, proved its worth and helped to point us in the right direction. On this basis, it proved possible to continue building up the Christian community even amid the ruins of an era and in an officially atheistic society.

With their impressive liberality, Jasper's ideas seemed almost dream-like in comparison — almost too beautiful to be true behind the drawn curtains of the Stalinist era. Yet I could never forget the philosopher's warning voice, particularly as day by day we were confronted with the pressures of an absolutized ideology too painfully to let us ever underestimate the dangers of every claim to absoluteness. Jasper's analysis of the exclusivity syndrome continued to be extremely relevant — even and above all as a challenging question to us as theologians. In our zeal for truth, where do we stand on tolerance? If our theological zeal for truth makes us unwilling to listen to these questions and work at them in a self-critical spirit, this zeal for truth will all too easily turn into that blind "zeal without knowledge" against which the apostle warns us. We have to be careful to avoid not only the Scylla of non-commitment in the matter of truth but also the Charybdis of intolerance. The little ship of theology and the church must be steered safely along the narrow course between the rock of an intolerant zeal for truth, on the one side, and the whirlpool of a tolerance without zeal for truth, on the other.

64   *Christ and Prometheus?*

NOTES

¹ *Vyklad viry*, c.5 (Czech: "Exposition of Faith").

² On the dialectic of the "exclusivity" and "inclusivity" of salvation, see my book *Reconciliation and Liberation: Challenging a One-Dimensional View of Salvation*, Belfast, Dublin, Ottawa, Christian Journals Ltd, 1980; and Philadelphia, Fortress Press, 1980, especially pp.33ff.

³ E. Hassinger, *Religiöse Toleranz im 16. Jahrhundert*, Basle, 1966, p.6.

⁴ This Toleration Edict, published in autumn 1781, granted the remnants of the severely persecuted Evangelical Christians in Bohemia and Moravia (and in the whole territory of the Hapsburg monarchy) the limited freedom to practice their religion publicly.

⁵ Cf. W. Kaegi, *Castellio und die Anfänge der Toleranz*, Basel, 1953, and H.R. Guggisberg, *Sebastian Castellio im Urteil seiner Nachwelt vom Späthumanismus bis zur Aufklärung*, Basel, 1956.

⁶ Quoted by E. Hassinger, *op. cit.*, p.20. The French could be rendered: "There is only one letter difference between 'reunite' and 'ruinate'." The justification of this warning has frequently been confirmed. After the Revocation of the Edict of Nantes, for example, war minister Vauban estimated, in a memoir, that "by the persecution of the Huguenots, France has lost 100,000 habitants, 60 million in cash, 9,000 sailors, 12,000 trained soldiers and 600 officers" (quoted by E.G. Rüsch, *Toleranz*, Zurich, 1955, p.20).

⁷ "Toleranz", in *Evang. Kirchenlexikon*, 4th ed., Stuttgart, 1963, col. 1247.

⁸ R. Ullmann in his booklet *Tolerance and Intolerable*, 6. In another context, H. Marcuse asserts that "the telos of tolerance is truth" (*Kritik der reinen Toleranz*, Frankfurt/M, 1967, p.102). Marcuse's criticism of "pure" tolerance, i.e. one which neutralizes all differences and decisions and therefore glorifies the status quo in society, provides food for thought. He sounds too dogmatic, however, when he offers as a general principle his positive directive: "A liberating tolerance, therefore, would mean being intolerant of right-wing movements and indulgent towards left-wing movements" (*op. cit.*, p.120).

⁹ *Das Evangelium des Johannes*, Göttingen, 1941, p.288.

¹⁰ *Kirchliche Dogmatik*, IV/3, Zürich, 1959, p.762. Cf. English translation: *Church Dogmatics*, IV/3, Edinburgh, p.665.

¹¹ "How My Mind Has Changed", in *Christian Century*, 20 September 1939.

¹² *Der Philosophische Glaube*, 6th ed., München, 1974, p.69.

6.
Kingdom, Church and World:
the Identity of the Pilgrim People of God

The transition from East to West does indeed confront a theologian with manifold challenges. In some respects it is a real crisis. Facing the challenges, I received substantial help through my participation in the ecumenical movement. That movement is full of tensions. Some of the particularly painful ones will be mentioned in the next chapter. But the ecumenical movement is also full of promise. The tensions can be lived out within the open horizon of the common Christian vision transcending divisions of confessions, cultures and societies. Here the identity of the people of God proves to be more than a pious dream.

Between the Assemblies of the World Council of Churches in Uppsala (1968) and Nairobi (1975) I was a member of both its Central and Executive Committees (and for a longer period chairman of the theological department of the World Alliance of Reformed Churches). Before that I was active, from Czechoslovakia, in the Working Committee of the WCC's Sub-unit on Church and Society; and later, from Switzerland, in the Standing Committee of the Faith and Order Commission.

I felt privileged that I was able to work exactly in these two areas of ecumenical involvement: "Church and Society" and "Faith and Order". They represent the vital interests and commitments of my theological pilgrimage and delineate the two aspects of my quest for theological identity: the theological and the ethical, the doctrinal and the social concerns of Christian faith. Sometimes the two elements are played against each other. How often was I involved in ecumenical debates between the "verticalists" and the "horizontalists", the one highlighting the transcendent and the other the immanent dimension of our faith! Yet in an authentic ecumenical (and theological) "geometry of salvation", the two dimensions belong together as the two beams in the cross of Christ. The goals of working towards the "Unity of the Church" and the

"Renewal of Human Community" should be distinguished but not separated. The "pilgrim people of God", oriented towards the kingdom, find their identity in fostering both these goals — in East and West.

Wanderers who love both earth and God

> We are otherworldly, or we are secular — but in either case this means we no longer believe in God's kingdom. We are hostile to the earth because we want to be better than the earth, or we are hostile to God because he deprives us of the earth, our mother; we seek refuge from the power of the earth, or we plant ourselves stubbornly and firmly upon it — but in either case we are not the wanderers who love the earth that bears them. Wanderers who love the earth aright do so only because it is on this earth that they make their approach to that alien land which they love above all else, except for which they would not be wandering at all. Only wanderers of this kind, who love both earth and God at the same time, can believe in the kingdom of God.[1]

Taken from an address given in 1932, these words of Dietrich Bonhoeffer are a memorable description of one of the fields of tension within which the central theme of the kingdom of God is set for the Christian community (and for Christian theology). This dialectic, which is quite fundamental for the biblical theme of the kingdom of God, can be threatened or even neutralized from two sides. Bonhoeffer describes both temptations. In the first place the kingdom of God can be taken to mean a reality which is utterly other, a transcendent other world beyond this one. In the pious radiance of this otherworldly reality, the earth pales into insignificance and ultimately becomes meaningless, hardly worth the religious person's commitment. The kingdom of God has nothing at all to do with the "labyrinth of the world" but everything to do with the "paradise of the heart". In that kingdom we can take refuge from earthly disappointments and tribulations.

This piety of other-worldliness and inwardness is not difficult to comprehend from our human standpoint. Situations arise in our earthly life — personal and social — when the pressure of circumstances and the burden of anxiety become so intense that people feel that only in that way can they attain some transcendent comfort in a comfortless world. Such comfort can be had fairly easily and is always to hand. "Whenever life begins to become oppressive and troublesome a person just leaps into the air with a bold kick and soars relieved and unencumbered into so-called eternal fields."[2] This "trampoline effect" is not to be mistaken for biblical faith in the kingdom of God. On the contrary, it comes within the scope of Karl Marx's well-known words: "Religion is the sigh of the oppressed creature, the sentiment of a heartless world and the soul of soulless conditions. It is the opium of the people."[3]

Tendencies to interpret the kingdom of God in otherworldly terms are matched at the opposite extreme by tendencies to interpret it in *secular* terms. There is no betrayal of the earth here. Earthly conditions and the responsibility of Christians for shaping them are taken seriously. Efforts are made to "work for the kingdom of God" and much may even be achieved in that direction. That is not to be despised; quite the contrary. But this approach becomes the "secularist *temptation*" when the kingdom of God is consciously or unconsciously identified with some earthly goal or other, and the goal of the kingdom of God entrusted to the care of the church. We build God's kingdom: we are the architects not only of our own future but also of God's. On this basis, our plans and achievements are sanctified. It is not that the kingdom of God comes but that we come into the kingdom.

Both these dead-ends in the interpretation of the kingdom of God — that of privatization and that of precipitate secularization — are to be avoided. But how are we to find another, a "third way" to interpret the kingdom of God, a responsible description of the relationship between the reality of God and our earthly reality in church and the world?

In the quotation from Bonhoeffer the theme of "wandering" or "pilgrimage" appears twice. It is stated that such pilgrimage accords with the kingdom of God only when the wanderer "loves both earth and God at the same time". The theme of "pilgrimage" with the kingdom of God as goal and standpoint reminds me of the historical church heritage which has a particular importance for me: that of the Czech Reformation. In that tradition the guiding vision of the kingdom, together with the personal and social commitment that vision entails, plays a particular role, more prominent than in the sixteenth century Reformation, and indeed retains that role from start to finish. Let me give just one example, that of Jan Amos Comenius, the last great thinker of the Czech Reformation. He was, in a literal and very painful sense, a wanderer, one who for the larger part of his life was a refugee. "I have been a wanderer all my life long. I have no home. It has been a restless, continuous enforced moving on from place to place with never a fixed abode anywhere. But now already I see my heavenly home."[4] This pilgrimage to the heavenly goal, however, this journey from "the labyrinth of the world into the paradise of the heart" (to use the title of one of the best known of Comenius's works) was in no way an escape into privacy but rather an almost inconceivably multiform effort to achieve the reformation and a humane renewal of secular and ecclesiastical conditions in education, church and society. In the midst of this labyrinth of the world, hope in the kingdom is to be demonstrated in persistent humane initiatives and projects.

The mystery of the kingdom

We must try to clarify the theme of the kingdom of God in terms of its contents. To see how necessary such a clarification is we have only to consider how often in the history of the church and the world this central thought of Jesus has been understood as a general concept. Certainly it is not just in the history of theology and the church that this theme of the kingdom of God plays an important role. It is a theme which has been emphatically present also in the history of Western philosophy and culture. We have only to consult Ernst Staehelin's seven volumes on "The Proclamation of the Kingdom of God in the Church of Jesus Christ"[5] to see how many variations there have been in the interpretation of this theme. I need only recall here the names of Hobbes and Locke, Lessing and Kant, Herder and Hegel — and there are countless others. When set alongside its biblical origin, the treatment of the theme here can be seen to be often extremely free and even arbitrary. We frequently get the impression that the "concept" of the kingdom of God is being used here as an "empty vessel" which we are at liberty to fill with contents of our own choosing in accordance with our own priorities.

There is no need for theologians to indulge immediately in vehement protests at such use or misuse of the message of the kingdom. This very diversity is itself a reminder that the kingdom is not something to be monopolized by the church but rather a reality which transcends the bounds of the church. This, moreover, as we shall see, is entirely in accord with the original thrust of the theme itself. Many a truly humane initiative has been launched with the kingdom of God as its inspiration, even along unaccustomed ways. But the task of theology is and will always be persistently to draw attention to the New Testament contents of this theme. In the Bible, the kingdom of God is not a protean concept. It has a distinctive shape which is embodied and delineated in the history of Jesus of Nazareth. Origen was right when he defined the kingdom of God as the autobasileia of Jesus Christ. And even Marcion, the great heretic of the ancient church, was right when he summed up the same insight in his dictum: *In evangelio est Dei regnum Christus ipse* (In the gospel, Christ himself is the kingdom of God), as quoted by Tertullian (Adv. Marc. iv, 33). If we are to understand the second petition of the Lord's prayer biblically, this is the direction in which we must look. When we do so, the message, the deeds and the fate of Jesus assume decisive importance.

Jesus' *message* is basically the good news of the coming kingdom, of the liberating promise and claim of that kingdom."If the whole of the New Testament is Gospel, this is the Gospel of the Kingdom of God."[6] We need only think of the parables, almost all of which are centred on the mystery of the kingdom; or of the Sermon on the Mount, which is surely no other than the covenantal constitution and directives of the kingdom. Still more important, not only the words of Jesus but also his deeds make the kingdom of God a present reality. I am thinking of his healing miracles: these were understood as signs of the kingdom, not only by outsiders but also by Jesus himself: "If I by the finger of God cast out demons, then the kingdom of God has indeed come upon you" (Luke 11:20ff.). Further, the rule of God is realized not only in the action of Jesus but also in his Easter destiny, in his cross and resurrection. The unmistakable view of the New Testament is that on the way of the man of Nazareth from the manger to the cross and to the empty tomb, the kingdom of God has drawn nigh to us. "Jesus comes in and with his kingdom."[7] Calvin rightly comments: "But when Christ could be pointed out with the finger, the kingdom of God was opened."[8]

It is not easy to describe more vividly the idea and the reality of the kingdom of God as intended by Jesus. No "definition" is possible. The words (and the person) of Jesus militate against doing so. It is surely significant that Jesus spoke of the kingdom mainly in parables, i.e. in a form of disclosure which is conscious from the very outset of its provisional character, indeed, which deliberately veils the mystery of the kingdom of God (in the sense of Mark 4:11) at the same time as it discloses that mystery. This surely means that we never have full grasp of this mystery. In attempting to sketch it we confine ourselves to one or two pointers.

In the New Testament witness to the kingdom, two apparently quite heterogeneous strands are combined. In the one strand, the *basileia tou theou* is understood, so to speak, in spatial terms, analogously (if also in emphatic contrast) to territorial kingdoms. The characteristic terms point in this direction: one can enter the kingdom (Matt. 5:20; 7:21; 18:3, etc.) and one can be thrown out of it (Matt. 16:19), and it can be shut against human beings by other human beings (Matt. 23:14). The images of a house or a city are evoked. This has a very concrete application — in the parables, for example, they speak of the house of the Father, the house of the King, to which people are invited, and in which they are regarded and treated as members of the household.

This understanding of the kingdom of God, this "strand" of the message of Jesus, is largely new. Only peripherally in the Old Testament does the expression appear in a similar sense. But there is the "other strand". The *basileia tou theou* can be understood as God's "sovereignty" or "kingly rule". This understanding is anchored deeply and centrally in the Old Testament. The Old Testament witnesses know that Yahweh is the true King of Israel and praise Yahweh as such. "Yahweh will reign for ever and ever!" (Ex. 15:18) is a credal affirmation which remains valid even if Israel chooses earthly kings in the manner of heathen nations. When this happened, it was not without hesitations and evident embarrassment, since it was feared, with good grounds, that the monarchy would mean rejection of the true kingship of God (1 Sam. 8). Yet the prophets kept alive the memory of Israel's true King in times of national decline in particular. And not just the memory; they also kept alive the hope of God's kingly rule, and did so indeed with an ever clearer eschatological vision. God indeed already sits on the throne today as yesterday, but the complete revelation of God's rule is still to come. God has the final word. The future belongs to God.

The prophetic message of the liberating sovereignty of God is fully taken up in the words and deeds of Jesus. Without the eschatological note bound up with it, the way of Jesus cannot be understood at all. The presupposition of his teaching and healing is that the final decisive hour has already arrived: "The kingdom of God is at hand" (Mark 1:15). And the New Testament witnesses with their diverse voices unanimously confirm in their experience of Easter that this presupposition holds good and that in the person and history of Jesus of Nazareth the sovereignty of God has once and for all "become flesh" definitively. In him God's kingdom was — and is — "in our midst" (Luke 17:21).

These two sets of ideas connected with the idea of the kingdom of God in the New Testament — i.e. the vividly concrete spatial and everyday one on the one hand, and the confession of Christ's royal sovereignty which points to the final future on the other — delineate the field of tension of the biblical theme of the kingdom of God. The tension between the two strands is quite fundamental for the New Testament understanding of the world, distinguishing it moreover from other eschatological and apocalyptic concepts of time. It "has stripped the idea of the coming world of the characteristics of apocalyptic fantasy and mystical indeterminacy, and has given it the imminent reality of an historical event... God's apocalyptically unique and eternal reality and his historically unique activity are regarded as an event which happens here and now and in the future."[9]

The judgment and the promise

What consequences does the kingdom of God as event have for the biblical view of the church and the world, and for the ordering of our life? The key statement of the message of Jesus indicates the way: "The kingdom of God is at hand, repent and believe the gospel" (Mark 1:15). The indicative of the first sentence here is matched by the imperative of the second. The decisive concepts are "repentance", or better still, "conversion" (*metanoia*) and "faith".

It is instructive that the first word of the "appropriate" response to the coming kingdom should be the word conversion. This is anything but obvious. As has already been pointed out, in the history of the interpretation of the kingdom of God the idea has all too easily been understood as a prolongation of human ideals, the ultimate climax of human aspiration. The New Testament takes a quite different view. Far from being the climax of our ideals or good-hearted intentions, the kingdom of God passes a sovereign *judgment* on them, i.e. it calls for conversion. The kingdom is certainly much more than a polemical concept. It does nevertheless have its dissociative polemical dimension. Augustine was not mistaken in contrasting his *civitas dei* with his *civitas diaboli*. This contrast exists even if we find it impossible to accept the philosophy of history underlying Augustine's statement. It is a sobering thought — yet one essential to a biblically responsible view — that the kingdom theme goes against the grain of our history to the extent that the latter is the history of our interests or, to use Marx's terms, to the extent that it is the history of the class struggle — which to a large extent it is.

This problem rightly receives a good deal of attention from Karl Barth in the final chapter of his interpretation of the Lord's prayer in the unfinished ethical section of the fourth volume of his *Church Dogmatics*. In this final chapter he is in fact dealing with the petition "Thy kingdom come!" He speaks of "the lordless powers" and here mainly in a critical perspective. What does Barth mean by "the lordless powers"?

The root of all evil is the destruction of the cosmic order by our human rebellion against the Creator. There is a paradoxical aspect to the tragic consequences of this rebellion: "Parallel to the history of humanity's emancipation from God there now runs that of the emancipation of humanity's own possibilities of life from humanity itself: the history of the overpowering of humanity's desires, aspirations and will by the far superior power of humanity's ability."[10] As with the spirits in Goethe's *The Sorcerer's Apprentice*, we become the prey of the "lordless powers", which we have unleashed: we are no longer their masters, but they have become ours. So it is that human beings, the autonomous "movers", are always at the same time becoming the "moved". We can only speak of this state of things, this entanglement in the world of evil, in mythological terms and the Bible does so by means of the vocabulary which the apostle uses — extremely impressively — in Ephesians 6:10ff.

The stark connection between such mythologizing discourse and the realities of our world can still be made clear and concrete even today (and perhaps especially today). Barth offers a number of examples. He refers to the myth of the state, to the exaggeration and even absolutizing of its power which turns the instrument of cooperative human order into an apparatus of blind domination and oppression. He recalls the destructive power of Mammon, the free play of vast interests concerned with profit, to which countless human beings — especially those at the bottom of society, but, in the last analysis, also those in leading positions — fall victim. But Barth also mentions the perverting sovereignty of the ideologies which so often try to force the human beings who create them into the Procrustean bed of their dictates and in this way to deform them. Barth views critically the "chthonic forces" beginning with the power of technology which, while liberating humanity, at the same time threatens and dominates humanity (today Barth would also be able to demonstrate this even more persuasively by reference to the increasing destruction of the human environment); and even the more harmless "powers" such as sport and even fashion.

What is operative everywhere here is the related strategy, the same pattern of alienation: the potentialities and powers invested in the creation and in humanity as part of this creation are turned by our human rebellion against the Creator into false absolutes and are even absolutized in opposition to humanity. This strategy of alienation has brought us today to the very brink of the ultimate historical danger — in the shape of accumulation and supremely dangerous "autonomizing" of the unimaginable arms potential, a development which we must today add to Barth's analysis as its ultimate critical culmination.

It is to this sombre background that the prayer for the coming of God's kingdom is related; it is into this dark abyss that it reaches. In this respect it is the first step of conversion and, in this sense, really the one thing needful. If rebellion against our Creator marks the beginning of the disease, the turning to God in prayer and intercession marks the beginning of the cure. A beginning which must be followed by sober factual analyses of the alienation mechanisms (of the kind Karl Marx furnished for dealing with an economy dominated by the profit motive) and by unstinting practical political efforts to find alternatives. The fact remains that, for the Christian, the prayer for the coming of the kingdom is the beginning, in the sense of setting out in a new direction; this is the first step in conversion.

But the message of the kingdom of God is not only the summons to conversion; it is at the same time the summons to faith: "... and believe the gospel!" The kingdom of God is much more than an everlasting critical authority; it is not just a warning light at the entrance to our individual and social dead ends. The gospel of the kingdom is certainly soberly aware of the reality of judgment and entertains no illusions on this score; it makes no secret of the seriousness of our human decisions; yet it does not do this wavering between "yes" and "no", light and darkness, but as gospel, as *good* news, bringing hope with it. By its very nature, the kingdom of God is the light, the light of Advent — *adveniat regnum tuum*! It is the word of promise and the reality of the promise, the invitation to faith and to life in the light of the promise.

How does this affect our understanding of the world and the way we order our lives? In my attempt to answer this question I want to refer to a central New Testament passage which has also remarkably accompanied the ecumenical movement on its way, namely, to "Jesus' first sermon" according to Luke 4:14-21. The fact that this passage provides the Lucan parallel to Mark's summary of the beginning of Jesus' ministry enhances its relevance for our theme. The core of the passage is as follows:

> The Spirit of the Lord is upon me, because he has anointed me to preach good news to the poor. He has sent me to proclaim release to the captives and recovering of sight to the blind, to set at liberty those who are oppressed, to proclaim the acceptable year of the Lord.

This is a quotation from the prophet Isaiah; it is the basic affirmation of Israel's hope, the promise of God's liberating and reconciling future. On this text Jesus preaches his sermon, which is reproduced in succinct form in the statement: "Today this scripture has been fulfilled in your hearing." It is a short sermon yet one in which the entire programme of the kingdom of God is indicated. Jesus declares that what Isaiah has promised as God's final messianic future is now operative. The hope of reconciliation and deliverance is not a distant song of the far future, utopian and remote from reality. The promises invade our relationships and circumstances.

The way opens up to a new relation to reality. Not some enthusiastic or fanatical way. Our actual circumstances are treated seriously. We are struck here by the sharp delineation of the various constraints and dangers in the world of humankind. Neither Isaiah nor Jesus soars off into the heavenly heights; both of them point down into the depths of the altogether real circumstances oppressing us all. The human beings who suffer, groups and individuals, are named; *the poor*, those who have come off badly in life, economically for example, the starving and the unemployed, but also in a moral or religious sense, the despised, the ignored, those cut off by the official church and society and considered suspect; then *the captives*, the prisoners, the people who have gone under or gone astray and are now at the mercy, or mercilessness, of rulers and the privileged; the servants and slaves, robbed of their freedom and rights as human beings. Then *the blind*, the physically and mentally disabled, the sick whose capacities for living are impaired, and *the oppressed*, the bruised: people whom life has broken because it has dealt them a bitter blow, or else because of personal failures and inner disintegration. All these people are present in this text; the whole human race, every single one in his or her particular need. Evidently, Jesus did not ignore the circumstances and pressures of the time; on the contrary, he names them by name: poverty, injustice, sickness, oppression and brokenness.

In the light of the kingdom, however, this unvarnished view of our world is not the whole of reality: the whole human race, each of us in his or her need — but *not* in fact on our own, *not* left to our own devices, *not* abandoned to the naked superior force of circumstances, but indeed placed within the light of the promise. What Jesus, like the prophet, promises is: to the poor — good news; to the captives — release; to the blind — recovery of sight; to the oppressed — liberty and salvation. In short, if human distress takes many forms, so does the promise of God.

This, then, is the relation of the kingdom of God to earthly realities. It approaches these realities in as earthly a way as could possibly be imagined: biologically, economically, historically and materially. But never as isolated realities, never on their own, never elevated to the status of some immutable inviolate fundamental law of reality: no biologism, therefore; no economism, therefore; no historical material-ism, therefore. For the world in which we live is not just its circumstances but always also the promises related to them. While the reality of the kingdom cannot be detected by any radar or understood by any computer, it is nevertheless present in the risen Christ and claims us and — above all — liberates us and sets us moving in the direction indicated by the promises.

Discipleship of the kingdom consists in attempts patiently and persis-tently to match human circumstances with promises and promises with human circumstances. This continues to be an urgent and relevant task down to our present time. The horizons of our world are darkening today. If we were to take only circumstances into account, only "the world as it is", the only honest reckoning would be an alarming and depressing one. The poet is right:

> To want the world to stay as it is
> is to want it not to stay at all. [11]

It is precisely here, however, that we should and can pray: Thy kingdom come! This is a "word of defiance". Certainly not one which wipes out as if by magic the oppressive circumstances but one which brings them within the operative field of the kingdom of God and thereby relativizes them and robs them of their seeming ultimate validity. *Kyrios Christos* — the Risen One is Lord of the "powers and authorities". This news liberates. We are no longer prisoners of an omnipotent fate. Our world does not have to "stay as it is". Resistance is possible. Our hearts and our circumstances can be changed. We are no longer completely at the mercy of sinful entanglements and destructive structures. Our task is patiently to dismantle them and to direct our steps towards the coming kingdom.

It makes all the difference to any civilization and society if there are within it groups of human beings who, in face of the tribulations of their time, keep their eyes steadily on the kingdom of God by praying for its coming, by being its disciples, especially in the direction indicated by Christ's promises: advocating the cause of the poor, serving prisoners and the disabled, raising up the oppressed and broken, and, above all, proclaiming the "acceptable year of the Lord", God's liberating future.

Pilgrim people of God: unity and renewal

These groups of witnesses of the kingdom of God who try to "love both earth and God at the same time" are Christians (although not exclusively so), the pilgrim people of God, the church. But in the perspective of the kingdom they never appear alone, never in isolation, but always in company with countless human beings who take quite different ways, with their fellow human beings in their particular concrete world. This raises the question of how the kingdom relates to these two groups, the question of church and world in the light of the kingdom. I now turn to look at this question. I shall do so by focusing primarily on the two ecumenical key themes of unity and renewal.

1. Unity

So far, in trying to outline the relationship of the kingdom of God to the reality of our world, I have spoken in a unitary way, without distinguishing between church and world. This was justified since, in the horizon of the kingdom, church and world appear in their fundamental, or rather, *eschatological* togetherness. It should be noted that this is no undifferentiated, ontologically stabilized and monolithic unity. It is no premature amalgamation and confusion between church and world. There is a legitimate concern for the inalienable identity of the church. We must take to heart what was said in Vancouver: "It is only a church which goes out from its eucharistic centre, strengthened by word and sacrament and thus strengthened in its own identity, resolved to become what it is, that can take the world on to its agenda."[12] In the course of history we must still go on making the distinction: the church is not the world and the world does not become the church. The unity between them can only be recognized and practised dialectically in hope, i.e. in the light of the kingdom. In that light, however, this unity is in fact promised and acquires a binding reality. "The church can go out to the edges of society, not fearful of being distorted or confused by the world's agenda, but confident and capable of recognizing that God is already there."[13] For the kingdom is not only the church's future but also the world's as well. In God's protological and eschatological plan of salvation, it is impossible to separate church and world.

This dialectic of the unity of church and world has been stated in exemplary fashion by Yves Congar:

> In God's unitary design the Church and the world are both ordered to this Kingdom in the end, but by different ways and on different accounts. Church and world have the same end, but only the same *ultimate* end. That they should have the same end is due to God's unitary plan and to the fact that the whole cosmos is united with man in a shared destiny. That they should have only the same *ultimate* end prevents a confusion that would be bad for the Church, as raising a risk of dissolving her own proper mission in that of history, and bad for the world, as raising a risk of misunderstanding and hindering its own proper development.[14]

This view accords with the specific dynamic of the biblical theme of the kingdom of God. Jesus' message of the coming kingdom is addressed primarily and unmistakably to the disciples. They are called "the sons of the kingdom" (Matt. 8:12); they are spoken of as "those invited" or as "guests" at the marriage feast (Matt. 22:3,8f.). Special communion with the kingdom's King is promised them; they are permitted to "sit at table" in the kingdom (Matt. 8:11), to "eat and drink" with the kingdom's King (Luke 22:30), to celebrate the marriage feast (Matt. 22:1-14; 25:1-15). Yet this special relationship of the group of disciples to the kingdom does not turn them into a closed society. The church has no monopoly on the kingdom of God. In contrast to certain tendencies within Judaism (or in the Qumran movement), the emphasis of Jesus is on the breaking of the firmly established barriers between, for example, the people of Israel and other nations — often indeed with a cutting polemic against "those born into the inheritance", "the sons of the kingdom". "I tell you, many will come from east and west and sit at table with Abraham, Isaac, and Jacob in the kingdom of Heaven, while the sons of the kingdom will be thrown into the outer darkness" (Matt. 8:11f.). The kingdom of God is clearly not under the management of hereditary administrators. What characterizes the "basic constitution of the kingdom" is Jesus' unmistakable practical concern for those who are excluded and discriminated against, his invitation to the "weary and heavy laden" (Matt. 11:28) and his table fellowship with notorious sinners (Matt. 9:10; Luke 5:29). Citizenship in the kingdom never means an arbitrary privilege but always a summons to discipleship and therefore to solidarity with people near and far.

Certainly it is possible to get this all wrong. Misunderstandings were already present in the company of Jesus' first disciples. The special intimacy of their commission was very soon transformed into a special claim: they coveted places of honour in the kingdom (cf. Matt. 20:21). This confusion, moreover, continues in the history of the church, despite Jesus' clear warning. There is one powerful, perhaps even the *chief*, temptation of church history: the temptation for the church to claim the kingdom for itself, to take over the management of the kingdom and even to present itself as the realized kingdom of God over against the world. Post-Constantinian Christendom, in particular, has been full of attempts and temptations of this kind.

In the light of the New Testament, all such attempts and temptations are to be firmly resisted. The kingdom is not the kingdom of Christians. Christians may and should live, act and suffer with this kingdom of God as their goal and celebrate its presence eucharistically. That is the "special feature", the "distinctively Christian" dimension of the church's existence. But Christians cannot ignore the fact that what appears on the horizons of the kingdom of God is not a church without the world but the new heavens and the new earth, the new creation. In the vision of the kingdom of God, the unity of the church is never an end in itself but always basically oriented towards the renewal of the human community.

2. Renewal

For Christians, the renewal of the human community begins in the church. Asked in what sense the church is the people of the kingdom of God, Jürgen Moltmann answers:

> The church in the power of the Spirit is not yet the kingdom of God, but it is its anticipation in history. Christianity is not yet the new creation, but it is the working of the Spirit of the new creation. Christianity is not yet the new mankind but it is its vanguard, in resistance to deadly introversion and in self-giving and representation for man's future. [15]

We should note the strong *pneumatological* emphasis here. It is entirely justified. For it is certainly no accident that, in the Nicene and the Apostles' Creed, the theme of the (one) church and of the (coming) world is dealt with in the pneumatological-eschatological Third Article. It is in the same direction that Paul points when he says: "*The kingdom of God is...* righteousness and peace and joy *in the Holy Spirit*" (Rom. 14:17).

The pneumatological emphasis in the vision of the kingdom helps us to avoid all immobility in defining the relationship between the kingdom of God, church, and world. As the power of renewal, the Holy Spirit is a dynamic reality. And, determined by the Spirit, unity will not be understood as a state but confirmed as a dynamic process, one related in fact to renewal. Just as in the vision of the kingdom of God church and world are inseparable, so too unity and renewal are inseparable from one another in the perspective of the Holy Spirit.

Unless I am much mistaken, this is the view taken by the New Testament. "For by one Spirit we were all baptized into one body — Jews or Greeks, slaves or free — and all were made to drink of one Spirit" (1 Cor. 12:13). I find these words particularly helpful in the light they throw on the field of tension denoted by Spirit, church, world, especially in their two dialectical emphases.

Firstly, the Holy Spirit places us in this concrete community, the church. The Spirit of Jesus is not a free-floating world soul, not a shapeless "cosmopolitan". He is the spirit of his community. We cannot simply ignore this community, indeed are forbidden to do so. One can, one will perhaps in some cases, be deeply pained by it; this was frequently the experience even of the apostle Paul. This community is no elite of the human race, not a "brilliant people" in the sense that it is culturally or morally superior.

"Not many of you were wise according to worldly standards, not many were powerful, not many were of noble birth..." (1 Cor. 1:26). Yet this human — only too human — community of faith is obviously the "object" of the Holy Spirit's working. The church becomes for us "the place assigned to us by the Spirit".

Secondly, however, another emphasis is to be noted: the fact that the church is the place assigned to us by the Spirit does not mean that we simply accept the concrete community of faith positivistically and resign ourselves to its actual mode of life. The Spirit of Christ is not a prisoner of Christ's body, as if his sole task were to maintain it in its existing form, but rather he seeks to mould it in the direction of renewal. The direction of this renewal is marked out by Paul as binding: the one Spirit of which we have all been made to drink binds us with our fellow human beings across all given frontiers and gulfs. It is surely not accidental that some of the most serious obstacles and rifts between human beings which are barriers to the achievement of unity — cultural, social and religious — are referred to in the apostolic passage just quoted. The Spirit combats these barriers and gulfs. While it is true that the Spirit blows where it wills, it is clearly in this direction that the Spirit is determined to blow — to overcome obstacles and to tear down barriers which keep human beings apart and sooner or later lead them to oppose one another, so as to renew human community. Every form of "apartheid" is sin — indeed, in this concrete sense, sin against the Holy Spirit.

It is in the church that the renewal of human community begins for Christians. At the same time, in the power of the Spirit, the church leads them (along with itself) beyond itself. Another classical New Testament passage on the Spirit, Romans 8, claims our close attention here. In a most impressive way, this passage combines the personal and ecumenical dimensions of the biblical witness to the Spirit. The Spirit comes to aid us in our weakness, "pleads for us" in the midst of our most intimate spiritual need, when we "do not even know what it is right for us to pray for" (v.26). Rooted in the vicarious action of the Spirit, however, this inner freedom sets us free for our fellow human beings, indeed, for our fellow-creatures generally. It is not just a question of the new human existence of Christians but of the new creation. The Holy Spirit does not reach the Spirit's final goal in the church — not even in a truly ecumenical catholic church. Paul describes this "open-endedness" of the Spirit poured out on Christians by using a remarkable image and speaking of the "first fruits of the Spirit" which we Christians already have (v.23). In other words, as Christians we have not got a corner of the Holy Spirit; the Spirit is not a predicate of Christian existence, still less a monopoly of Christians. It is counter to its very nature for this "first fruits of the Spirit" to be commandeered and misused for selfish needs of our own. On the contrary, it is characteristic of it to open our eyes and hands to the "eager expectation of the creation", to the threat of annihilation which affects the whole created world as well, including that part of it outside the church (v.19ff).

> The new creation of man by the Spirit is not a flight of faith into heaven or an abandonment of this imperfect world... On the contrary, the new creation means beginning to see the world as it is, suffering with it and taking its suffering to heart... The work of the Spirit is to make us aware of our solidarity with the world.[16]

The Holy Spirit leads — in the light of the kingdom of God — into a fellowship with "the whole creation" in its destiny and its hope. The only consistent response to the movement of the Spirit, therefore, is an all-inclusive ecumenical view of the world and practical solidarity on the part of ecumenical Christendom which strives for unity and renewal.

> The hour when the church today prays for the coming of God's kingdom drives it for better or worse into the company of the earthlings and worldlings, into a compact to be faithful to the earth, to its distress, its hunger, and its dying.[17]

NOTES

[1] D. Bonhoeffer, "Thy Kingdom Come", in *Preface to Bonhoeffer*, ed. J. Godsey, Philadelphia, Fortress Press, 1965, p.28.

[2] *Ibid.*

[3] *Early Writings*, McGraw-Hill, 1964, p.43.

[4] *Unum necessarium*, X,10.

[5] *Die Verkündigung des Reiches Gottes in der Kirche Jesu Christi — Zeugnisse aus allen Jahrhunderten und allen Konfessionen*, Basel, Reinhardt, 1951-1964.

[6] K.L. Schmidt, in *Theological Dictionary of the New Testament*, ed. Kittel, Vol. 1, p.583.

[7] Joh. Schneider, *ibid.*, Vol. 2, p.670.

[8] *Institutio religionis christianae* (1559), II, 11,5.

[9] E. Lohmeyer, *The Lord's Prayer*, pp.99-100.

[10] Karl Barth, *The Christian Life*, 1981, p.214.

[11] Erich Fried, a poem called "Status quo zur Zeit des Wettrüstens".

[12] *Gathered for Life*, official report of the Sixth Assembly of the World Council of Churches, Vancouver 1983, ed. D. Gill, Geneva, WCC, 1983, p.50.

[13] *Ibid.*

[14] *Lay People in the Church*, Bloomsbury Publishing Co. Ltd, 1957, p.88.

[15] *The Church in the Power of the Spirit*, London, SCM Press Ltd, 1977, p.196.

[16] Eduard Schweizer, *The Holy Spirit*, Philadelphia, Fortress Press, 1980, pp.109-110.

[17] D. Bonhoeffer, *op. cit.*

7.
Human Rights:
Ecumenical Identity in a Divided World

One of the test cases of our quest for theological identity in East and West is the burning issue of human rights. Here the ecumenical dimension of the identity issue is of utmost importance. The alert observer of the ecumenical scene can hardly fail to notice that human rights have been moving into the centre of ecumenical interest.

I have been personally involved in these activities, particularly as moderator of the study programme of the World Alliance of the Reformed Churches, but also by supporting the Czechoslovak human rights movement "Chart 77" promulgated by my teacher, Prof. Jan Patocka, and by participating in the UNESCO project on religion and human rights.

In all these areas I had soon to go through a sobering experience: the special actuality and the growth of the ecumenical preoccupation with human rights does not mean that there is any clearly defined agreement as to how vital questions should be tackled, where the emphasis should be placed, how priorities should be determined, or even how, in general, human rights should be understood and safeguarded. On the contrary, in facing the sensitive problem, the differences of perspectives and emphases became frustratingly apparent. There has hardly been a topic that evoked so passionate and bitter reactions within the ecumenical community as the question of human rights. I recall the deadlock at the Assembly of the WCC in Nairobi 1975. Here our ecumenical identity is painfully put on trial.

Challenge to the churches

We live in a world echoing in all directions with reports of poverty, hunger and misery, of exploitation and oppression of great masses of people, of the arrests, torture, and assassinations of politically undesirable persons, of the abduction of innocent people by politically radical revolutionary groups or by greedy robbers, of the suppression of any freedom of expression by dictatorial regimes, including the freedom to confess one's own religious belief — of any number of incidents, in other words, which reveal a frightfully widespread disdain for and degradation of human personhood. In such a world, a deep disturbance of conscience drives us to seek possibilities for the protection of fellow men and women who are being treated or are being physically and psychologically injured in these ways. [1]

These words by Prof. Ludwig Raiser, a Tübingen scholar of constitutional law and a committed Christian, bring out the context of our worldwide struggle for human rights. The situation is not a completely new one. What is relatively new, however, is the massive escalation of dangers and atrocities as well as the growing awareness of them due to the continuous stream of information through the mass media.

The concept is helpful, in both its parts. The adjective points to the fact that the manifold degradation of persons and nations is not only a matter of those directly involved but a universal, i.e. truly "human" concern. The substantive "rights" indicates that the problems have not only their personal and moral dimension but constitute a legal and political issue as well. What is demanded is not only a private and individual response, but also an institutional and international one. The Universal Declaration of Human Rights (1948) and the Human Rights Covenants of the United Nations (1966) were important steps in this direction.

The acute human rights problem is a major challenge to ecumenical Christianity. Certainly, Christians have no monopoly in this field. On the contrary, the churches' record is a rather ambiguous one. Different historical and confessional stages can be distinguished. Charles Wackenheim, a Roman Catholic theologian, ventures the following hypothesis:

> The message of Jesus and of the primitive church helped to give men a powerful awareness of their true dignity. During the first three centuries of the Christian era, the church ceaselessly asserted the rights of man and this in the face of the imperial power. After 313, the need for the cohesion and survival of human institutions took precedence over the proclamation of "the truth that makes men free" (John 8:32). Once she gained the social and cultural leadership of the West, the Roman church espoused as a matter of course the ideology of the established order. From this point of view the claim for individual rights appeared subversive. [2]

It has taken a long time for the churches to learn their human rights lesson. [3] Today, there is a serious endeavour to "pay the historical debt" in this respect. For the Roman Catholic Church, Vatican II marked a breakthrough. "By virtue of the Gospel entrusted to her, the Church proclaims the rights of man (*iura hominum*); she recognizes and highly values the contemporary dynamism which is giving a new impetus to these rights everywhere."[4] Responding to this thesis, the papal commission Iustitia et Pax has continuously addressed itself to the theological and practical issues of human rights and published the results of its work.[5]

On the Protestant and Orthodox side, for years the World Council of Churches has concerned itself with the problems of human rights and finds itself again and again at breaking point over the concrete implications of the issue.[6] The confessional world bodies, particularly the World Alliance of Reformed Churches[7] and the Lutheran World Federation,[8] have also been at work on the subject for a considerable time. It would seem, in fact, that church circles have recognized human rights as "kairos", God-given challenge/opportunity, for the church. In consequence, theological literature on the subject has steadily grown.[9]

Human rights in a divided world

Of course this striking ecumenical convergence of interest does not mean that there is any automatic agreement as to issues and processes. The question of human rights presents itself to us in a divided world, and in consequence the contemporary understanding of human rights itself betrays this "divided" character. We hear often today of the "three worlds": the Western capitalist world, the Eastern socialist world, and the third world consisting of the developing countries. Human rights are understood in different ways in each of these three worlds.

In the *Western* view of human rights, the centuries of tradition behind it, the rights of the individual, with his/her inalienable dignity and certain classical prerogatives, stand in the foreground: freedom of belief and conscience, the equality of citizens before the law, legal protection for the citizen against any encroachment by the state, the right to property. The insistence on such rights can be easily understood on historical grounds. They grew up in the struggle for the rights of citizens over and against traditional political and ecclesiastical institutions — in the struggle, that is, which, though it is anchored deep down in the history of Western society, produced its most decisive results at the time of the American and French Revolutions, when the bourgeoisie came into its own. The classical declarations on human rights bear the marks of this origin: they protect the interests of citizens as free individuals, free producers, free property-owners.

Socialist-communist concepts of human rights are opposed to this individualistic approach and its bourgeois-capitalist outworking. Not that the intention to safeguard human dignity is in any way disputed in the socialist view, but it is more concretely conceived and more practically worked out through the establishment of social relationships which make it possible for all people, especially the hitherto underprivileged, to enjoy their personal, political and cultural as well as their economic and social rights. This is held to be possible only in a socialist society. Hence the socialist view of human rights is determined by the objectives of the socialist society. The interests of private persons are subordinated to the rights of society.

How does the question of human rights appear from the viewpoint of the *third world*? It is not really possible at the present time to speak of a unified doctrine of human rights in the third world. Nevertheless the priorities of these countries are clear: the basic need for survival in face of the famines which threaten so many; the dismantling of colonial structures; the overcoming of racial discrimination; the achievement of cultural authenticity. The rights of individuals pale into insignificance in the light of these collective needs. The primary human right in such circumstances is the right to work and eat; the right to greater equality of opportunity between poor and rich; the right to the ending of exploitation at national and international levels.

These concepts of human rights are not, when properly understood, mutually exclusive. But it is not always easy, amid the realities of world politics, to see how they complement each other. Far from leading to harmony, they bring tension and conflict. There are frequent clashes between the different points of view in public debate and in the discussions of international bodies.

Pure ideology?

Is the concept of any practical use? Does the notion of human rights have any common meaning or basis? Is it not rather, in its ambiguity, a typical ideological weapon — a smoke-screen to conceal vested interests?

Such sceptical questionings of the contemporary human rights debate are strongly voiced by the political and ideological representatives of the "second world". This fact may be illustrated by the negative reactions of Soviet ecclesiastical representatives to discussions on human rights in the World Council of Churches, and by the way in which the concept of human rights was placed under taboo at some international conferences. All this does not simply result from present conditions on the political scene. The critical attitude towards human rights has a deeper historical dimension in the Marxist-socialist heritage.

Even in his younger days, Karl Marx saw the ideal of human rights in bourgeois society as a misleading expression of the self-interest of the "haves", the questionable "right of the strong" at work within the class society. In other words it was for him an ideological formulation of the bourgeois worship of mammon. He wrote: "Nothing in these so-called human rights goes beyond egoistic man — that is, beyond man as a part of bourgeois society, an individual turned in upon himself, upon his own private interest and his own private whims and fancies, and alienated from the wider community." Such an abstract ideal could never meet the real needs of people, but would rather gloss them over. "Man has not been liberated from religion. He has simply gained religious liberty. He has not been set free from property. He has gained freedom to own property."[10] Behind the noble ideal of human rights lay, in short, one single interest: that of the possessor.

It is clear from the way in which Marx identifies religion directly with class-conditioned egoism that he himself is arguing from a narrow ideological standpoint. Nevertheless his critical observation that egoistic man is hovering menacingly in the background whenever human rights are discussed remains critically relevant and topical. Christians must be prepared for self-criticism at this point as they consider both church history and the present situation. How often the churches have engaged themselves actively and resourcefully on behalf of human rights only when their own interests were involved, their own power and influence at stake! Or how hard church people have found it to bestir themselves, say in the matter of religious liberty, when it has not been the freedom of their own confession but that of others which has been at issue! Even in the second half of the nineteenth century, Pius IX could categorically condemn the following proposition: "Any human being is free to embrace and profess the religion which the light of reason has led him to judge to be the true one."[11] It will do Christian theologians good therefore to reflect on Marx's criticism and apply it to themselves — for the sake of their credibility and so of the effectiveness of their present-day concern for human rights.

We can also learn something from Marx to help us give a positive answer to the question whether a human rights programme has to do with anything more than an ideology. He forces us to check that any given stand for human rights is not just limited to one's own interests but takes into account the rights of one's fellow people and commits itself to them — that it "goes beyond egoistic man". This "going beyond" — understood in a Christian way, in terms of concrete obligation, as Jesus Christ

himself understood it — becomes the criterion, and marks our passage
from the ideological to the theological struggle for human rights.

Learning ecumenically

Along this line, an ecumenical "learning process" has developed in
recent years. This has produced some positive results, in spite of halting
progress and occasional setbacks. Not that in this field ecumenical
understanding among Christians comes easily. Ecumenical debates, like
those in the world political arena, are affected and encumbered by the
differing concepts and interests of the "three worlds". This state of
affairs is illustrated by the passion which discussions about human rights
in the world church have constantly aroused. Their common faith does
not save Christians from being caught up in the conflicts of their world.
Rather, it is in the very midst of these conflicts that their faith is put to
the test. And yet, in spite of everything, the *common* faith survives amid
all the tensions. Here lies the hope of ecumenical Christianity. The
conflicts do not go away. But they are seen in the light of a common
foundation and a common goal. In this way rigid positions become more
flexible. Thus there are opened up, in every human predicament,
possibilities of ecumenical understanding and cooperation — possibilities which should not be underestimated even against the background of world politics.

The brief history of ecumenical discussions on human rights illus-
trates this possibility. There were many twists and turns in its course. It
could be said that the most striking change has been the shift from the
almost self-evident dominance of the Western-liberal view at the
beginning to the later acceptance of socialist criticism and the third
world's concern with living standards. This process has often shown
sudden shifts of emphasis. Thus many participants from Western
countries were asking themselves, in the light of the debates at the
World Council of Churches particularly in the period between the
Assemblies in Uppsala 1968 and Nairobi 1975, whether the pendulum
has not swung too far in the direction of socialist and third-world
concepts. In the heat of the struggle against racism in the first and third
worlds, was not too little attention being paid to the classical question of
religious freedom in the second world?

The World Council took notice of these questionings. The dialogue
about human rights was intensified, and the ecumenical context helped to
overcome the danger of seeing the problem in terms of false alternatives.
The consultation on "Human Rights and Christian Responsibility", which

took place in 1974 in St Pölten, Austria, for example, in spite of many tensions, produced some positive results in the attempt to work out a broader concept of human rights. This is shown by the following "Analysis of Fundamental Human Rights":

a) There is a fundamental right to live, involving the whole question of survival, of the threats and violations which result from unjust industrial, social and political systems, and of the quality of life.
b) Men (sic) have a right to enjoy and preserve their cultural identity — a right which embraces such questions as national self-determination, the rights of minorities, and so forth.
c) Men have a right to take part in decision-making within society — a right which involves the whole question of effective democracy.
d) Men have a right to hold different opinions — a right which preserves a society or a system from hardening into authoritarian rigidity.
e) Men have a right to personal dignity — which implies, for example, the condemnation of torture and of excessively prolonged imprisonment without trial.
f) Men have a right to make a free choice of belief and religion — which implies freedom to practise that belief or religion, either alone or in fellowship with others, in public or private, through teaching, practical activity, worship and the performance of rites. [12]

The consultation referred to this "definition" as "a common basis". The description is justified to the extent that in this ecumenical catalogue of human rights a realistic consensus over the differing, yet inter-related human rights was achieved. Its consolidation, and wherever possible its development, are among the most pressing future tasks in the ecumenical struggle over human rights. Let me indicate more concretely two dimensions of this task, the "horizontal" and the "vertical".

Complementarity, comprehensiveness, universality

It would be a misunderstanding of the ecumenical consensus on the complex nature of the concept of human rights if we were to conceive it simply in terms of a pluralistic complementarity: as though each "world", not to say each individual, having its own needs and interests, should be able to express them freely and be happy "in its own fashion". Such a standpoint would correspond to the ideology of "egoistic man". We must never confuse it with a theological theory and practice of human rights based on the normative "word and event" of Jesus Christ. Jesus of Nazareth, as we find him in the New Testament, is, in his unreserved offering of himself to God and his fellow-human beings, the very antithesis of egoistic man. The salvation he brings is open for all; it affects soul and body, the individual and society, humankind and "groaning creation" (Rom. 8:19).

The complexity of the concept of human rights in the world of today must be understood theologically in the light of what we know of Christ: not in the sense of a stabilizing tension between opposing interests, but in terms of their dynamic relationship with each other. It is right and proper that in the different "worlds" people should fix their priorities and draw protection and strength from them at those points at which their humanity is especially threatened and oppressed. Thus in a bourgeois-capitalist world those socio-economic rights which are so often undervalued must be constantly brought to mind (participation of workers in industry, the right to work, etc.). On the other side, in a Marxist-communist society a stand must be taken for the underdeveloped rights of freedom of belief and conscience. Yet in every legitimate engagement for human rights Christians will always be encouraged, by remembering the all-embracing salvation in Christ and the ecumenical horizon of faith, to look and go beyond their own particular standpoint and to respect the rights of others with their different priorities. In any case the playing-off of one's own interests against those of others — so often practised in the political world-stage — should be ecumenically resisted. As I see it, the particular task of the church in this field is that of outgoing towards others; to bear in mind the indivisibility of human rights in our divided world; and so to be "counsel for the defence of our fellow's rights" (for us in the industrial countries that would mean, for example, defending the vital interests of the third world).

This insight into the complementarity, comprehensiveness and universality of human rights has its primary application in a spatial, geographical sense — keeping the ecumenical horizon open over one's own region and one's own world. But it has also a temporal dimension. It has to do with the interdependence of the generations in history. The rights of our contemporaries are not the only frame of reference for a responsible theory and practice of human rights. The way we exercise our rights affects the opportunities and rights of future generations. They must all therefore be coordinated. Every conscious or unconscious adoption of the *après nous le déluge* stance, whether by individuals or groups, perverts our human rights into human wrongs. This is, notoriously, the strategy of "egoistic man". This temporal aspect takes a special urgency today in view of our relations with our environment. Such an understanding of human rights leads us to strive not only for economic but also for ecological justice. By its redemptive and ecumenical character, faith in Christ lays on the Christian a special responsibility in this respect too.

Human rights before God

We thus come to the "vertical" aspect of the theological understanding of human rights: to the question of its significance in the context of faith in God. Christian thinking, as well as secular thinking, sometimes shows great reserve at this point. The argument is this: human rights concern everybody; therefore we should avoid overstressing a definitely theological or specifically Christian view, so as not to set ourselves apart from other people. In reply we must ask: Can there be a theological understanding of humanity which leaves God out of account? And is it true that to emphasize the "distinctively Christian" must necessarily involve separating oneself from others? For myself, I would answer both these questions in the negative, and insist on the importance of the idea of God, formulated in a Christian sense, for an ecumenical understanding of human rights.

Theoretically, for overcoming a too-ready acceptance of received arguments for human rights (especially perhaps the traditional liberal ones), Christian theology has in the past often called for such acceptance and has shared the limitations and prejudices associated with such "rights", particularly their individualism and idealism, and their anthropological optimism. This tendency must today be corrected and a wider approach adopted. At this point the biblical notion of God, which concerns itself with the totality of creation and its needs, offers a liberating, open horizon. In a theological sense, human rights are in no way to be defined or constituted either as predicates of nature or some timeless "essential humanity", or as the result of some historical-materialistic process of self-deliverance. Theologically the right to be human must be anchored in a real answerability *coram Deo* (before God).

This theoretical anchoring leads to an important ethical consequence, because it resists any particularistic narrowing of the concern for human rights. The formulation *coram Deo* has "the advantage that it respects, and demands respect for, the dignity and rights of all men and women. By contrast any formulation based on experience must necessarily be limiting and selective, because our experience is limited and we can only conceive of what is universally human by the extrapolation of what "human" means for us.[13] The common reference to God and God's kingdom is of the utmost importance because it gives the ecumenical commitment to human rights its openness and its sense of obligation.

Finally we must mention the inner potential of faith in God as personal motivation in the quest for human rights. In practice this quest is threatened from two sides: in the first place by the discouraging setbacks which are so often experienced; and in the second by the rising spectre of self-righteousness which can corrupt the best intentions. Here our knowledge of the "vertical dimension" comes to our aid, bringing both encouragement and rebuke. It saves us — to quote the document from the World Alliance of Reformed Churches — "from despairing in situations of overwhelming and frustrating setbacks... At the same time, it prevents our involvement in the struggle for human rights from becoming a self-righteous justification by works rather than a thoroughgoing repentance and self-giving investment in justice and freedom as a response to our having been justified by God's grace alone."[14]

Understood in this way, a clearly articulated theological reference and the emphasis on a Christian perspective on human rights are not to be taken as implying an "ecclesiastical go-it-alone", or a "Christian solo-run" in the highly-charged field of human rights, much less as pleading for "the preservation of Christian privileges". On the contrary, the "distinctively Christian", understood in the biblical sense, establishes no privileges, but drives us, as we follow Jesus, to an unconditional openness and commitment to others.

Fundamental motivation

What is the material Christian motivation for ecumenical commitment to the cause of human rights? Many answers to this question can be given by quoting and interpreting concrete passages from the Old and New Testament. Even when we have to recognize that the concept of human rights is a modern one and that it cannot be mechanically derived from the Bible, prophetic and apostolic texts inspire and support the concern for human dignity leading eventually to the formulations of human rights. Yet such a concern is rooted not only in some occasional biblical quotations but in the fundamentals of Christian thought. Christian faith is the faith in the Triune God, the God of our creation, salvation and eschatological hope. All three "fundamental articles" of the apostolic faith motivate Christian engagement in the field of human rights.

a) The Bible speaks of the one God, the *Creator* of heaven and earth. God's name is proclaimed with special intensity by God's own people, yet God does not belong to a particular nation or church. God is the Creator of all men and women. On the first page of the Bible, in the creation story, we read the classical statement: "God created man in his own image, in the image of God he created him; male and female he created them" (Gen. 1:28). This is the fundamental human condition: all other definitions and conditions are secondary compared with this primary one. In this is grounded the ultimate dignity of human beings. All creatures with human face participate in it. As such, it is inalienable. It is independent of all possible differences among human groups — sexual, racial, national, social, religious. These differences are real. Yet they are secondary. They must not be absolutized and/or misused for justifying the special superiority of one sex, race, class, culture over another. It was only logical that some of the first attempts at codifications of human rights like the "Virginia Bill of Rights" (1776) made their appeal to the one Creator.

Contemporary ecumenical documents generally agree in emphasizing the "image of God" motive and try to elaborate its importance for a theological concept of human rights. For example in the "theological guidelines" of the World Alliance of Reformed Churches we read:

> In the identification of our humanity as created in the image of God, we affirm:
> — the equal dignity and interdependence of man and woman;
> — the equal validity and interdependence of personal rights (freedom and dignity) and social rights (justice and community);
> — and the equal dignity and interdependence of the present generation and future generations in the stewardship of nature.
> As humanity stands in a covenant relationship to God, that relationship carries with it covenant responsibilities in our stewardship of creation.
> Further we acknowledge:
> — the equal validity and interdependence of "my rights" and "the rights of my neighbour"; and
> — the equal significance and interdependence of human rights and human duties. [15]

b) The central place of Christian confession, its heart, belongs to God's story of salvation in the message and destiny of Jesus of Nazareth. The "logic" of this story — the reason why it happened — is given in the most important of ecumenical creeds with the words "for us human beings and for our salvation". This is indeed the overall tendency of Jesus' life. "The Son of man came to seek and to save the lost" (Luke 19:10). His way is that of unconditional solidarity with all human beings with particular emphasis on those marginalized and discriminated against: the poor, the sick, the religiously ignored, the women, the children... His first sermon, the "programme for his mission", deals with the fulfilment of the old prophetic vision: the Lord "has anointed me to preach the good news to the poor. He has sent me to proclaim release to the captives and recovering of sight to the blind, to set at liberty those who are oppressed, to proclaim the acceptable year of the Lord" (Luke 4:18f.).

What do these emphases in Jesus' words and activities mean for a movement towards human rights? "Normally the traits we have just named are simply classified as products of the decisive factor or Jesus' 'compassionate love'. This is to diminish their significance. Jesus' attitude is a significant demonstration, to show that these very persons who are ignored, despised and defamed by society, have a right to recognition, to show that there is an inalienable dignity of man, a right to which also the 'sinner', the outcast, the criminal, are entitled. With this attitude Jesus is bearing witness to the fact that, as Kant puts it, he recognizes man not as the 'means' but as the 'end' in itself, and that Jesus sees in each and every person creatures loved by God, and by seeing people in this light he is thereby honouring mankind in its humanity. There is absolutely no distinction at this point between human rights and human dignity."[16]

The apostle Paul grasped this fundamental tendency of the salvation in Christ correctly when he formulated: "There is neither Jew nor Greek, there is neither slave nor free, there is neither male nor female; for you are all one in Christ Jesus" (Gal. 3:28). It is true that the liberating impact of this programme was not fully understood and still less implemented by Christians in the church and society. We can only repeat: the churches' human rights record is ambiguous. Yet it is also true that the ecclesial and social challenge involved in Paul's words has never been completely silenced. It presses for bolder steps towards more effective implementation of its liberating potential. It still has its future.

c) The fundamental element of Christian faith is its future-oriented dimension. The God of the Bible is the God of eschatological hope. The word "eschatological" points beyond history, transcends all human achievements, opens the transcendent reality of the "kingdom of God". Yet that transcendent reality is not simply detached from our historical situation. "The kingdom of God is in your midst" (Luke 17:21). The parables of Jesus confront the promises of the eschatological kingdom — its vision of ultimate salvation and liberation — with the everyday circumstances of our life. The hope of the kingdom encourages our active response in history. Transcendence becomes the power of immanence. It de-fatalizes historical conditions. It empowers us never to give up and always to seek for a *plus ultra* of justice and freedom in the light of the coming kingdom.

What does this mean for Christian understanding of human rights? Paul gives a good example. He was well aware of the importance of his civil rights. When confronted with false accusations, he did not hesitate to appeal to the emperor or remind his adversaries of his Roman citizenship. Yet the same Paul, imprisoned and deprived of his rights for the time being, writes to his fellow believers: "Our citizenship is in heaven" (Phil. 3:20). This is an essential Christian emphasis. It is good to know that there is a fundamental human right which cannot be taken away from us, not even in the situation of persecution and oppression. At the same time, this liberating "heavenly citizenship" makes us concerned about the state of our "earthly citizenships", enlarging the horizon of our struggle for yet unrealized human rights.

In this eschatological perspective, a Christian understanding pleads for a prospective character of human rights. We are genuinely grateful for many historical definitions and achievements in the struggle for human rights. We appreciate the attempts at their international codification in our times. Yet our endeavour cannot stop at the definitions of the past and the codifications of today. Not only because of those disturbing features and developments mentioned at the beginning of this chapter, but also as a matter of principle. "It has not yet appeared what we shall be" (1 John 3:2): the hope for humanity is greater that all its historical realizations, important as they truly are. We always may and should seek for a *plus ultra*. The human rights story is an "open-ended" process, full of dreams and frustrations, achievements and setbacks. Yet it is a process under the ultimate promise. Christians bear witness to that promise — joining hands and exchanging thoughts with people of other religions and ideologies to protect and to enhance our common human rights.

NOTES

[1] "Menschenrechte in einer gespaltenen Welt", in *Evangelische Kommentare*, Stuttgart, 1975, p.200.

[2] "The Theological Meaning of the Rights of Man", in *The Church and the Rights of Man*, A. Müller and N. Greinacher eds, New York, Seabury Press, 1979, p.52.

[3] There have always been Christian individuals and groups protesting against the prevailing obliviousness and short-sightedness of the churches. I think, for example, of Comenius (1592-1670) opposing the religious intolerance of his days: nobody has the right "to impose his principles (in philosophy, theology or politics) on anybody else, but, on the contrary, everyone should allow all other men to express their views openly and enjoy in peace what is theirs by right" (*De Rerum Humanarum Emendatione Consultatio Catholica, Panorthosia*, 8,2-3; extracts in Jeanne Hersch ed., *Birthright of Man*, Paris, Unesco, 1969, pp.249f.).

94   Christ and Prometheus?

[4] *Gaudium et spes*, 41, 3.

[5] *The Church and Human Rights*, Vatican City, 1975.

[6] *Human Rights and Christian Responsibility*, Vols 1-3, Geneva, WCC, 1975.

[7] Allen O. Miller ed., *Christian Declaration on Human Rights*, Grand Rapids, Eerdmans, 1977.

[8] *Theological Perspectives on Human Rights*, Geneva, Lutheran World Federation, 1977; also J. Lissner-A. Sovik, "A Lutheran Reader on Human Rights", in *Lutheran World*, 1978, pp.1-217.

[9] Cf. J.M. Lochman-J.Moltmann eds, *Gottesrecht und Menschenrechte*, Neukirchen, Neukirchener Verlag, 1976; W.Huber-H.E. Tödt, *Menschenrechte*, Stuttgart, Kreuz Verlag, 1977; J. Baur ed., *Zum Thema Menschenrechte: Theologische Versuche und Entwürfe*, Stuttgart, Calwer Verlag, 1977; A.Müller-N. Greinacher ed., *The Church and the Rights of Man*, New York, Seabury Press, 1979; A.D. Falconer ed., *Understanding Human Rights: an Interdisciplinary and Interfaith Study*, Dublin, Irish School of Ecumenics, 1980; G. Thils, *Droits de l'homme et perspectives chrétiennes*, Louvain, Publications de la Faculté de Théologie, 1981.

[10] *Die Frühschriften*, S. Landshut ed., Stuttgart, Kröner, 1953, pp.194,198.

[11] Syllabus, 1864, No. 15, in Denzinger Schönmeister, *Enchiridion Symbolorum*, Freiburg-Roma, 1965, p.2915.

[12] *Human Rights and Christian Responsibility*, *op. cit.*, p.61.

[13] J. Moltmann, in *Evang. Kommentare*, 1976, p.282.

[14] *Christian Declaration on Human Rights*, *op. cit.*, p.146.

[15] *Ibid.*, p.145.

[16] Josef Blank, in *The Church and the Rights of Man*, *op. cit.*, p.33.

8.
Apocalypse Tomorrow?
A Christian's Account of Hope

I began with a brief reflection on the concept of identity. I mentioned three different dimensions of the issue: anthropological, theological and ecumenical. There is one common element in all these if we try to understand them biblically. A Christian understanding of identity is characterized by its future-orientation and open-endedness. It is "identity in hope".

This has much to do with the fundamentally eschatological nature of biblical thought. Biblical scholars of our century rediscovered what was always present in the prophetic preaching and teaching of the church: the biblical witnesses lived, suffered and spoke in the perspective of the coming kingdom. They thought in the element of promise.

I have referred to this constitutive mark of Christian thinking in practically every chapter of this book. How strong was the eschatological fervour of the Czech Reformation! What would Christian existence in Eastern Europe be without the spirit of hope? The time of dialogue between Christians and Marxists was the time of hope and so is the time of ecumenical engagement. There is an unquenchable promise connected with the central theological themes raised: the biblical vision of truth, of God, of the kingdom.

In this concluding chapter hope will be articulated as the theme.

The crisis of hope

The theme of hope does not seem to be a fashionable ecumenical topic any more. In the sixties, the ecumenical preoccupation with hope found general backing in the spirit and mood of the times. In all the three worlds, there were hopeful signs of genuine renewal in many churches and societies, new opportunities for greater justice, freedom and participation. In 1968, the ecumenical boat sailing towards Uppsala under the banner of "Behold, I make all things new" took a good deal of cultural wind into its sails. In the seventies, however, the climate changed and that changed mood has continued into the eighties. Too many attempts at reform and renewal had been suppressed. Too many hopes had ended in disappointment.

Today the question of the future presents itself in a whole range of challenges which must be dealt with if there is to be any future at all. I name only the most important ones: poverty and hunger, by which the majority of our contemporaries are deprived of even the most elementary necessities of life; economic exploitation both in individual countries and on a world scale; racist, political and ideological oppression, and the denial of human rights in many areas of the world; the threat to the world itself by the massive accumulation of the weapons of mass destruction and as a consequence of the rapidly expanding human capacity for disturbing and devastating our natural environment; and the creeping nihilism of meaningless life-styles in the midst of otherwise privileged, prosperous and consumer-oriented societies.

These seem to be the "apocalyptic times": no wonder that the last book of the Bible gets new attention, particularly its dark and terrifying pages. An apocalyptic language is to be heard not only in the apocalyptically minded sects but also in political proclamations. Apocalypse now — or tomorrow?

There is another dimension to the crisis of hope today, a *challenge* not so much from the outside but *from within* the reflection on hope. There are some contemporaries who question not only particular hopes but hope itself as a legitimate human attitude.

Let me mention a particularly moving example for me personally. A few years ago I received the posthumous papers of the Czech philosopher Vitezslav Gardavsky. He was one of the Marxist participants in the Christian-Marxist dialogue in the sixties. He achieved fame with his book *God is Not Entirely Dead* (1967) in which he developed a very positive interpretation of biblical thought from a Marxist standpoint. For him the figure of Jacob represented the creative model of humanity venturing to transcend all the historical, cultural and religious boundaries in quest of richer human possibilities — a model of dynamic hope. Written in the seventies, the posthumous papers confront us with an entirely different perspective. Gardavsky did not lose his interest in the Bible. But it is no longer Jacob who is the key figure but rather the prophet Jeremiah, "the man of sorrow", in captivity, an outsider both politically and religiously. For Gardavsky, Jeremiah is the antipode not only to Jacob but also to

Prometheus, who is for him the mythological symbol at the roots of Western technocratic civilization in both its capitalist and Marxist versions. The disruptive nature of that civilization has become increasingly obvious. We need a critical look at that Promethean heritage, which has two constituent elements: the fire (technology) and "blind hope". It is the combination of the two which leads to disaster, the *plus ultra* drive of insatiable technocracy. Therefore the conversion we need in order to be saved in our societies and on our planet is from "blind hopes", and from hope altogether. Liberation from hope is a precondition of human wisdom and survival. Gardavsky pleads for creative hopelessness, not in the sense of fashionable nostalgia or despair but in the sense of patient and modest life-style stripped of aggressiveness and of illusions.

It is in this context of sharpened outward and inward challenge that we Christians are called to give "an account of our hope" (1 Pet. 3:15) today. It would be a meaningless undertaking if we were to disregard these challenges.

This undoubtedly increases the difficulty of our witness. When we try to speak of hope we run into cultural cross winds. However, there is also another side to this. The same critical situation offers us a positive opportunity: the chance to become more concerned and more precise about the real *ground* of the hope within us. In the days of facile hopes the churches are easily tempted to adapt their message of hope to the prevailing optimistic climate of their societies, to present their account of hope as one version of a general mood of hope. The biblical "salt" of hope then loses much of its specific flavour, its true "saltness". I would see here a chance offered to us in a changed situation: the radical challenge could lead us to seek a radical answer.

By radical we mean the New Testament ground of hope. The cultural environment of the New Testament was not one of facile hopes. It was dominated by a rather dismal, more or less fatalistic spirit. There were profound questionings as to the legitimacy of human hope as such. Today's challenges to Christian hope are therefore nothing new in the history of the church. They could bring us nearer to a better understanding of the background and, still more important, to the common ground of the apostolic hope.

As point of departure and focus, I wish to refer to one central text expressive of New Testament hope: *"That is why we struggle and work hard, because we have set our hope on the living God, who is the Saviour of all, especially of those who believe"* (1 Tim. 4:10). Three points seem to me to be of particular importance; (1) the ground of hope; (2) dimensions of hope; (3) hope and freedom, in action and in suffering.

The ground of hope

In the apostolic perspective there is no ambiguity whatever about the ground of hope: "We have set our hope on the living God." In clear contrast to its secular use, the New Testament word *elpis* does not mean a changeable "floating" attitude with an uncertain background. Christian hope is rooted neither in the potentialities of nature nor in the creativity of human history. It is not matter which is "the mother of hope" (E. Bloch). Still less is it the sum-total of human achievements or the quality of the religious consciousness. There are human expectations which can be built on such foundations and they have their due importance for human life. But hope in the biblical sense has a quite specific anchorage. Hope and God are inseparable: to be "without God in the world" means to be "without hope" (Eph. 2:12). The symbolism of the anchor as the sign of Christian hope rests concretely on one basis: "We have set our hope on the living God."

Several years ago I was invited by Korean theologians to a consultation in Seoul and asked to deal with the theme "Our Hope: God's Suffering in Human Struggle". At first I found this formulation bewildering. The inseparable connection between God and hope is expressed unambiguously: our hope is rooted in God's involvement in human *struggles*. The formulation goes further and elucidates the crucial and liberating way of God's involvement: participation in *suffering*. Does not such a formulation go too far? Should it not rather read: "God's struggle in human suffering"? Human suffering is indeed well-known to us — but God's suffering?

However, the Korean theologians were right. In this emphasis we undoubtedly encounter the heartbeat of the biblical faith in God. Already in the Old Testament the God of Israel was testified as the One who identifies, and suffers, with the people. And in the New Testament this understanding reaches its peak in the passion of Jesus Christ and in his death on the cross. Hence the cross is the distinguishing mark of the Christian concept of God. The "living God" of the apostolic message is the "com-passionate" God. If a concept of God is not capable of expressing this com-passion of God, it cannot be a Christian concept of God.

On this central point there was a parting of ways — already in the early church and actually throughout the whole history of Christian doctrine. The early church fathers were faced with an immensely difficult task in their philosophical environment. For the existing concepts — those of Greco-Roman antiquity — in no way fulfilled the necessary requirements. On the contrary. In their sublime philosophical-metaphysical emphasis they uncompromisingly excluded any com-passion and any capability of suffering on the part of God. God cannot suffer. God's metaphysical state is not compatible with suffering — and even less with com-passion. *Apatheia* is the basic attitude of the metaphysical God. The classical doctrine of God is developed under the premises of the "axiom of apathy".

The weight of this philosophical heritage burdened the Christian history of dogma. It was extremely difficult to fight this heritage. The Trinitarian concept of God played an important role in this spiritual struggle. [1] Sometimes, we have difficulties in understanding this concept. Yet Trinity means that God participates in our struggle, that God suffers in our struggles. In the Trinity the passion of Jesus Christ — the story of the Son, his struggle, his suffering — is taken up in the mystery of God's love. The implication of this is that God is not divorced from suffering, no apathetic being. God identifies with God's Son and through him with us. In this sense a true "revolution in the concept of God" occurs in Trinitarian thinking.

This "revolution" was very early and very often "softened" and neutralized, as so many authentically biblical ideas and motifs were. Today we have every reason to take up these impulses again and develop them. The theologians of the third world, particularly from Asia, have made a substantial ecumenical contribution in this respect. [2]

This task is not only valid in view of the authentic biblical origin of theology. It is also true in view of the special need of our witness in modern society. I am thinking of the necessary encounter with atheism. One of its especially poignant and challenging themes is the protest against God in the name of suffering creation. This theme is raised passionately (or silently) by Dostoyevsky or Camus, but also by many of our contemporaries. I consider this protest to be basically justified and appropriate. Theology and the church have every reason to listen to it understandingly. Such a listening is not possible, however, except in a self-critical way. Indeed has not Christian theology actually provoked this protest by advocating — against its better judgment — an apathetic concept of God? The passionate protest in the name of suffering creation is entirely in order facing an apathetic God. On this point evangelical Protestants can hardly do otherwise than align themselves with the atheistic protesters. "Without Jesus I would be an atheist" (Johannes Gottschick).

Jesus, and the belief in God which we gain from the story of his life and death, are quite different. In Jesus we encounter the God to whom no human suffering is foreign. To be confronted by this God in view of the suffering creation — and in one's own suffering — does not mean to be thrown into the deadly void of absolute apathy, but rather to experience the abundance of divine sympathy. The justified protest of the atheists does not really reach the living God. On the contrary, this God himself launched this protest against the powers of death in the Easter events by exposing himself to the attacks of death. Thus he restored the right of suffering creation and placed its destiny in the eschatological perspective of the hope of resurrection and liberation (Rom. 8:18ff.).

We have every reason not to hide this eschatological light under a bushel. It contains liberating power and potential, an element of the "nevertheless" even in apparently hopeless situations. The older Barth used to say that "to clasp the hands in prayer is the beginning of an uprising against the disorder of the world". He was right. To say "Yes!" to God in faith and hope means to say "No!" to death and its allies, the "principalities and powers" of sinful destruction and oppression. It is an invitation to act accordingly: "To struggle and to work hard" in hope.

The dimensions of hope

The second issue I would like to discuss briefly is the question of the dimensions of hope, of the range of hope. The apostolic affirmation I am referring to is the continuation of the previous words: "Who is the Saviour of all, especially of those who believe". At first glance, this looks like an example of awkward logic. It speaks first of "all" but then, as if afraid of its own boldness, it speaks "especially of some". Clearly it works with two accents, distinguishes two dimensions of the horizon of hope. But, precisely in this "open-ended" way, it is faithful to the dynamic characteristic of the New Testament treatment of the relation between church and world. In our accounting for hope, both aspects of this statement should be respected.

I start with the little word "especially". The biblical vision of hope is related especially to those *who believe*. When we were considering the "ground of hope" we already stressed that hope is not an abstract human virtue, a general predicate of the human psyche or of history. Hope and the living God — the Saviour — belong together. There is a sociological aspect to this. The "movement of hope" initiated in the name of the living God is not a chaotic *Sturm und Drang* ("storm and stress") but a structured and disciplined mission. It is rooted in the apostolic faith; it is carried out in the apostolic way. Hope, therefore, can neither be limited to a private inward matter of the isolated individual nor dissolved in cosmopolitan generalities. It initiates the "third way", that of a committed fellowship, of Christian brotherhood and sisterhood. God's vision and mission of hope calls forth a concrete human agency, the "people of God", the "people of hope": the church. For the God of hope is the Saviour *especially* of those who believe.

But it would be a misunderstanding of this apostolic "especially" if we were to isolate it from the preceding words *who is the Saviour of all*. The legitimate specialness of the church does not mean an exclusive privilege or even monopoly of hope. Established Christendom has throughout its history tended to draw such a conclusion; its representatives have presented themselves as the proprietors of hope and the managers of salvation. Such an attitude distorts the biblical concepts of both hope and salvation. In the New Testament there is no monopoly of hope. We find there the dynamics of the Spirit, and, above all, the dynamics of hope — inspiring believers to witness to hope and to serve hope. The "especially" applied to Christians confers no privilege of ownership but only the privilege of mission. This mission points beyond the boundaries of the church. The light of the eschatological hope reaches much further than the four walls of the church. It "radiates through them" and makes them transparent. The hope of Israel becomes the hope of all nations. In the ultimate New Testament perspective of hope, what appears is not a temple but the city of God and a new heaven and a new earth: the new creation (Rev. 21). The God of the believers is the God of all.

This dynamic tension between the apostolic "all" and the apostolic "especially" is also very important for our accounting for hope today. It corresponds to the dialectic emphasized in our chapter on "Kingdom, Church and World". It reminds us that we confess a hope which is entrusted in a special sense to the church, the hope of the church and for the church. Our accounting for hope would cut itself loose from its moorings and lose its credibility if it were to "float" in cosmopolitan (or vaguely ecumenical) clouds without manifest connection with the life of our actual churches. We are all aware that this is not at all easy. A glance at most of our churches, especially those in traditional and affluent countries, is far from encouraging. And yet: *Hic Rhodus, hic salta!* This is where the witness of hope begins: at the grassroots of hope, in our churches. Their present condition can be painful for us; we can struggle with them and about them; but we cannot give them up. To do so would be to lose the "home base" of hope. The presence of congregations of the people of God within a society and their witness to the name of the living God in that society make a difference to its spiritual and cultural climate.

At the same time, the apostolic "Saviour of all" reminds us of the radically open horizon of hope. The church is the cradle but not the tomb of hope; its base but not its prison. A merely ecclesial witness of hope would miss the dynamics of its theme. Here the ecumemical dimension and movement of hope become important — in its search both for the unity of the church and for the community of humankind. An account of hope which lacks a conscious relationship to a concrete local communion easily becomes empty; an account of hope without an ecumenical horizon easily becomes blind. The apostolic message can help us to face up to both these dangers.

Hope of freedom: in action and suffering

There is a third element in the apostolic message of hope: the witness to the ground of hope and the statement about the range of hope lead the apostle "to struggle and to work hard". This is a strong language: the Greek words refer to drudgery and to a life-and-death struggle (agony), to human action and to human suffering. The setting for the apostolic witness of hope is not conditions of good fortune and easy comfort. Hope opens up the narrow way of Christian freedom in action and suffering, especially in adverse situations.

Hope opens up the narrow way of freedom. It strikes me how often in recent ecumenical discussions the motif of hope is connected with the motif of freedom. It is no accident that the "ecumenical theology of hope" paved the way for the ecumenical "theology of liberation" (and vice versa). There is a biblical reason for this: for the witnesses of the New Testament (as indeed for the prophetic witnesses of the Old Testament) there is an intimate connection between the hope set on the living God and the practice of freedom. "That is why we struggle and work hard." Biblical salvation implies hope of freedom and freedom of hope.

When hope and freedom are so closely related, what does it mean for our understanding of both these terms? Two accents of the keyword "hope of freedom" must be distinguished and connected. First, in the biblical understanding of hope there is always an element of the "not yet". The life of a Christian in hope and freedom is no automatic progress and triumphal procession. It is a "narrow way" which is constantly menaced from within and without: hope in the struggle, freedom under the cross. It is striking that the central promises of salvation and liberation in the New Testament at the same time soberly declare the depth of the human predicament: "We know that the whole creation groans with pain like the pain of childbirth until now" (Rom. 8:22). And in Romans 7, with reference to the apostle's own life: "I see in my body another law... making me captive of the law of sin" (7:23). No doubt, the human world is, objectively and subjectively, a deeply estranged world. The idealists and the optimists are therefore mistaken when they argue: I ought, therefore I can. The real human condition is different: "I don't do the good I want to do; instead I do the evil I do not want to do... Wretched man that I am!" (Rom. 7:19,24). There is no euphoria of freedom in the New Testament. Freedom takes place in hope.

And yet, although the biblical vision of the human situation bars the way to easy-going idealism and optimism, in doing so it does not in any way direct us to enter the opposite camp of the pessimists and the "realists". I think of those programmes and attitudes which, seeing the conditions of human bondage and the risks of freedom, fatalistically freeze them, recommending authoritarian reactions and structures. Such a "realistic" philosophy and practice is incompatible with the Christian vision of hope. There is the other element in the biblical hope of freedom. There is not only the "not yet", there is also the "already" of the promise and the commitment of the living God. The apostolic message is clear about it — precisely in the passages which we quoted as reflecting the depth of the human predicament. The bondage of the creation is radical and universal — and yet it is oriented "towards hope" (Rom. 8:20). The sigh of Paul — "Wretched man that I am!" — is deep; and yet, it is not his last word; it is followed immediately by "Thanks be to God through Jesus Christ our Lord!" (Rom. 7:25). Humanity is not a *massa perditionis*, damned for all eternity, but it exists rather in all its predicament already "in hope", under the impact of God's salvation. There is a hope for freedom.

I am convinced that both the accents of hope just mentioned should shape our memory and our hope. The first aspect is already worth considering with its sobering "eschatological reservation". Under the conditions of history, the hope of liberation must always be seen as an open engagement but never as a perfected "kingdom of freedom" (Hegel, Marx). In church history, particularly in the secularized movements of Western Christianity, the lack of sober clarity on this score has been considerable. Engagements for progress and freedom have been hailed as the emerging secular salvation and, precisely because of it, corrupted. How often has a movement of liberation turned into an established repression! In many a freedom fighter of the past and present there appears a future oppressor. Ernst Bloch expressed this experience in 1930 in the following words: "In the *citoyen* there was a hidden *bourgeois*;

heaven forbid what's hidden in the 'comrade'!" (Christians should first ask rather what's hidden perhaps in the pious crusader!) This experience is not to be misused in a defeatist and even cynical way to point to the futility of all historical involvement. But it can be of positive service to this involvement if we remain sober and free in it, without absolutizing our cause and our achievements.

Even more important, perhaps, is the other, *positive* accent of hope. Unless I am very much mistaken, the real threat to freedom in our world comes not so much from the idealists of freedom but rather from the political fatalists and cynical despisers of freedom. True enough, they hold many trump cards in their hands: the prospects of freedom in the contemporary world are not all that bright. At the beginning of this chapter I mentioned a whole series of discouraging features. Armageddon ahead of us? Apocalypse tomorrow? No wonder that in many places there are growing tendencies towards fatalistic power-politics and corresponding feelings of the powerlessness and futility of all commitment.

In such a setting, a Christian witness of hope can prove as important and as relevant today as it did in the not so very dissimilar conditions and atmosphere of apostolic times. The apostolic hope was then and is now a *resistance movement against fatalism*. In the perspective of the living God's liberating involvement in the Christ event, fate is broken. The "principalities and powers" (Rom. 8:38) no longer possess the ultimate key to human and cosmic possibilities. They are powerful; sinful elements and oppressive structures in history must be taken seriously. But they are not omnipotent. They cannot "separate us from the love of God" (Rom. 8:39). We are not left alone in our struggles. God suffers and acts with us. There is hope for freedom and freedom for hope. That is why we do not need to be resigned — in spite of everything. The last word of biblical Apocalypse is: hope.

Very often, Christians living under overwhelming oppression and distress understand with clarity this relevance of the ultimate eschatological hope for our acting and suffering in history, and witness to it with credibility. I gave some examples from Eastern Europe. Let me conclude by pointing to Christians from the third world. One of my ecumenical assignments several years ago was to summarize and to introduce the "Ecumenical Account of Hope" for the meeting of the Faith and Order Commission in Bangalore (1978).[3] In my preparation for that assignment, I had the privilege to study a variety of the "Documents of Hope" from different ecumenical contexts. Some of those written in the situation of struggle and suffering were of particular importance for me. I shall never forget a testimony given by an imprisoned Latin American Christian. In the darkness of his cell he lives by the memory and hope of the cross and the resurrection. He appropriates the Easter message as the vision of the "unforbiddable Tomorrow". There are so many "forbiddable tomorrows" in our life: how many have been forbidden to Christians in Eastern Europe! How many are forbidden to our brethren and sisters in the third world! And how often every one of us hits a wall that separates us from a tomorrow of our plans and dreams — professionally, existentially, socially! A time in prison is a drastic expression of such situations. Yet exactly here, the hope of the resurrection liberates. It strengthens (to quote our Latin American brother) "the murmur that the victory of night is not complete". The dark threats of the Apocalypse have not the final say.

This account of a quest for theological identity seeks to strengthen that Christian murmur.

NOTES

[1] Cf. my study "The Trinity and Human Life", in *Theology*, Vol. 78, 1975, No.658, pp.173-183.

[2] Cf. K. Kitamori, *Die Theologie des Schmerzes Gottes*, Göttingen, Vandenhoeck & Ruprecht, 1972.

[3] Cf. the report *Bangalore 1978*, ed. Lukas Vischer, Geneva, WCC, 1978.